NATIONAL DEFENSE RESEARCH IN

T0274837

WHAT FACTORS CAUSE INDIVIDUALS TO

Reject Violent Extremism in Yemen?

Eric Robinson, Kate Frier, Kim Cragin,
Melissa A. Bradley, Daniel Egel,
Bryce Loidolt, Paul S. Steinberg

Prepared for Office of the Secretary of Defense
Approved for public release; distribution unlimited

For more information on this publication, visit www.rand.org/t/rr1727

Library of Congress Cataloging-in-Publication Data is available for this publication.

ISBN: 978-0-8330-9809-2

Published by the RAND Corporation, Santa Monica, Calif.

© Copyright 2017 RAND Corporation

RAND® is a registered trademark.

Support RAND
Make a tax-deductible charitable contribution at
www.rand.org/giving/contribute

www.rand.org

Contents

Protestors collect money in upturned umbrellas to be distributed to victims of violent clashes during protests against then-President Ali Abdullah Saleh, August 2011.

Figures and Tables

Summary

Why do some individuals become terrorists? Why do some choose to travel overseas to become foreign fighters and others remain home to engage in political violence? More than academic, the answers to these questions inform a central component of U.S. national security strategy: countering violent extremism. This report addresses the topic of radicalization—or individual motivations to engage in political violence—in Yemen. This report uses data from focus groups and a national survey conducted during the spring of 2016.

Yemen is in the midst of a civil war. In the wake of the collapse of the government of Tunisia in 2011, Yemeni protesters took to the streets in major cities to protest the reelection of then–President Ali Abdullah Saleh. After protracted negotiations by the Gulf Cooperation Council (GCC), Abd Rabbuh Mansur Hadi, who was Saleh's vice president, took over the presidency in February 2012. By then, the internal strife had gained momentum. The Houthis, who had fought several wars against Saleh's forces, had used the unrest to expand from their stronghold in the Sa'ada governorate. They eventually seized the capital of Sana'a in September 2014. President Hadi and his forces retreated to Aden and southern Yemen, but the Houthis pushed south and assaulted Aden's international airport in March 2015. The civil war had begun.

More than 10,000 people have died in Yemen's civil war. Nearly 2.2 million—out of a total population of 27 million—are internally displaced and an additional 200,000 are refugees overseas. Various nonstate armed groups exist. Some fight with the aforementioned Houthi movement. Others have joined the local al Qaeda affiliate, al Qaeda in the Arabian Peninsula (AQAP). Still, others are associated with the Islamic State. These armed groups fight against one another as well as the Yemeni military forces and those of the Arab coalition. With such a widespread conflict, it would be easy to understand the motivations of those who are sympathetic to, or become involved in, political violence. But rather than focus on support for political violence per se, the report looks at the other side of the coin—why individuals reject violent extremism in Yemen. It argues that the more effective approach to countering violent extremism is to reinforce a propensity toward nonviolence. Our key findings follow in the next section.

> **More than 10,000 people have died in Yemen's civil war. Nearly 2.2 million— out of a total population of 27 million— are internally displaced and an additional 200,000 are refugees overseas.**

Key Findings

- Choosing not to engage in violence is attitudinally distinct from opposing political violence in theory.

- Urban centers represent important populations for strengthening nonradicalization.

- Yemenis perceive attacks against local civilians as more legitimate than attacks against foreigners, including aid workers.

- Social ties, measured by the degree of influence exerted by family, friends, and religious leaders, also do not affect individual radicalization in one clear direction.

- Yemenis view political violence as a form of activism, so redirected pathways—or participation in nonviolent activism—do not diminish a propensity for violence.

Policy Implications

These key findings hold a number of implications for U.S. national strategy and countering violent extremism (CVE) programs. First, the survey asked respondents a series of questions to delineate (1) individuals who were unlikely to engage in violence from (2) those who opposed political violence in theory. We found that choosing not to engage in violence is attitudinally distinct from opposing violence: They represent two unique forms of nonradicalization. Logically, policy interventions that treat both forms of nonradicalization the same are less likely to be effective.

Second, the findings also suggest that urban centers represent key populations for both forms of nonradicalization, albeit in different ways. Respondents in urban centers were less likely to support travel overseas to fight against occupying forces and yet more likely to express a willingness to engage in violence. The implications are twofold: CVE programs aimed at minimizing support for foreign-fighter travel should focus on urban centers. The intent should be to build on existing opposition for traveling abroad to fight and help this opposition to spread into rural areas. Further, diplomacy should be used to reinforce the cessation of hostilities in urban centers by encouraging actors on the ground to avoid repressive security measures.

Third, survey participants viewed local attacks against Yemeni civilians as distinct from attacks against foreigners. In fact, respondents articulated greater support for attacks against Yemenis than foreigners. The finding suggests that Yemenis understand the civil war as a local conflict and, thus, have been less affected by the global rhetoric of al Qaeda or the Islamic State calling for attacks against foreign interests. We suggest that these results be verified with further research, considering that fieldwork for this report was conducted prior to an uptick in the pace of Arab coalition airstrikes in late 2016. That said, if the findings hold true, the policy implication is that Yemen represents less of a priority for the fight against such transregional networks as the Islamic State.

Fourth, the findings also suggest that social ties—as measured by the degree of influence exerted by family, friends, and religious leaders—drive underlying attitudes toward violence, but they have no clear effect on the choice to engage or not engage in violence. Why? The focus group discussants indicated that the ongoing conflict in Yemen has wrought a general distrust of social authority figures in that country. This general distrust, in turn, may have diminished the significance of social ties in Yemen when it comes to individual motivations and behavior as it relates to political violence. It represents a significant policy challenge: The U.S. government and the Arab coalition may struggle to find an abundance of "credible voices" within Yemeni society for CVE programs or even perhaps diplomatic efforts to reinforce the central government. This may limit the possibilities of what can be accomplished in the near term.

Finally, it is not uncommon for commentators to posit that one way to deal with the problem of radicalization is to provide an alternative outlet for grievances. Our conceptual framework identifies this idea as a "redirected pathway." The survey questionnaire asked a series of questions on political and social activism to gauge the importance of potential redirected pathways toward nonviolence. The findings suggest that redirected pathways do not diminish a propensity toward violence. In fact, the findings suggest that Yemenis view political violence along a spectrum of political activism. This finding should reinforce a general skepticism among U.S. policymakers that democratic reforms will strengthen nonradicalization in a direct and meaningful way, absent long-term social changes.

Abbreviations

AQAP	al Qaeda in the Arabian Peninsula
CVE	countering violent extremism
DEFF	design effect
EA	enumeration area
ESS	effective sample size
GCC	Gulf Cooperation Council
ICC	intracluster correlation coefficient
ME	margin of error
NSS	nominal sample size
OR	odds ratio
UAE	United Arab Emirates
UN	United Nations

Taiz governorate, Yemen.

CHAPTER ONE

Introduction

I n October 2000, 21-year-old Walid bin Attash played a critical role in al Qaeda's attack on the USS *Cole* while it refueled in the Yemeni port city of Aden. Attash had purchased the explosives and the boat used in the attack, which would take the lives of 17 American sailors and injure another 39.[1] Nearly a decade later, Shawki Ali Ahmed al-Badani—at age 31— became a leader and operative for al Qaeda in the Arabian Peninsula (AQAP) and organized attacks against the U.S. Embassy in Yemen's capital, Sana'a.[2] By 2012, the U.S. government viewed AQAP as a more dangerous threat to the homeland than al Qaeda Core in Pakistan.[3]

Why do some individuals, such as Attash and al-Badani, engage in political violence, while others do not? Why do some travel overseas to become foreign fighters and others remain home? These questions have puzzled academics and policymakers alike for decades.[4] And they are even more difficult to answer in such a country as Yemen, which is in the midst of a brutal civil war and has experienced multiple internal conflicts in the past 50 years—conflicts rife with ideological, social, political, and territorial cleavages.[5] Over the last two decades, Yemen has hosted al Qaeda fighters intent on attacking the United States and Western Europe, as well as American allies in the region. This complexity—the various layers of political violence embedded in Yemen's recent history—makes it difficult for experts to understand what motivates individuals in Yemen to engage in terrorist attacks at home and overseas.

This report addresses the topic of radicalization—or individual motivations to engage in political violence—as it relates to Yemen. As such, it addresses violence associated with Sunni tribal militias, Houthi militias, AQAP, and fighters linked to the Islamic State. Rather than focus on support for political violence per se, the report looks at the other side of the coin—why individuals reject violent extremism. To do this, it builds on a conceptual framework

> **Why do some individuals engage in political violence, while others do not?**

for nonradicalization published in prior iterations of this research and investigates this topic with data from focus groups and a national survey conducted in the midst of Yemen's ongoing civil war.

The report is third in a series on this subject. The first report—"Resisting Violent Extremism"—appeared as a journal article and presented a conceptual framework for why more individuals do not turn to violence to achieve their political goals. It argued that enough of a difference exists between factors that cause individuals to engage in terrorism and factors that discourage such activities that policymakers should treat responses separately.[6] The second report in the series—*What Factors Cause Youth to Reject Violent Extremism? Results of an Exploratory Analysis in the West Bank*—appeared as a report published by the RAND Corporation and, based on the conceptual framework presented in the journal article, addressed the topic of nonradicalization using semistructured interviews and a survey conducted in the Palestinian West Bank. It revealed that family played a greater role than friends in shaping attitudes toward nonviolence and, equally important, that opposing violence in theory was distinct from choosing not to engage in violence.[7]

This report, the third in the series, is a counterpart to the second one, using the same basic analysis construct (with focus groups and a survey) that we used in the West Bank to examine the unique case of Yemen. The country was chosen for several reasons. First, Yemen has experienced ongoing internal conflict for the past 50 years, which means opportunities abound for individuals to engage in political violence. Second, understanding the influence of AQAP on local populations is of interest to U.S. policymakers because the group has targeted the United States.[8] And third, the increased instability associated with Yemen's civil war means that few surveys have been conducted in the country over the past two years, making the findings of interest to a wider audience. For this report, researchers conducted six focus groups (three with men and three with women) with ten participants in each group in and around Sana'a, Yemen's capital. We also commissioned a national survey with representation in each of Yemen's six regions. The quantitative findings in this report draw on responses from the 1,200 individuals who participated in the cluster-based survey during a two-week period in May 2016.

This report has four main sections. The first provides a background discussion of the conflict in Yemen and the various terrorist groups operating in Yemen that have threatened the United States. The second section outlines the methods and data used to explore why individuals choose to reject political violence in Yemen. The third contains a detailed discussion of the qualitative and quantitative results. The report concludes with a discussion of the implications of those findings for U.S. counterterrorism policy, countering violent extremism (CVE) programs, and future research.

Readers should note that an appendix contained in this report also provides greater detail on our survey and sampling approach. This report does not include a summary of what scholars generally know (and do not know) about the structural causes of terrorism (referred to as "root causes") or individual radicalization. For those readers interested in these topics, refer to the previous two reports in this series for an in-depth discussion.[9]

Yemenis protest against then-President Ali Abdullah Saleh, August 2011.

CHAPTER TWO

Overview of Conflict and Instability in Yemen

Yemen, located on the Arabian Peninsula to the south of Saudi Arabia and with a population of approximately 27 million, is in the third year of a civil war. The civil war, which has been described by some as a proxy war pitting Iranian-backed Houthi forces in Yemen's northern governorates against Arab-backed forces in the south, has devastated the country. Beginning in March 2015, the civil war has already claimed the lives of an estimated 4,000–10,000 civilians, and upward of 6,000 fighters.[1] More than two million have been displaced from their homes by the conflict, and GDP has fallen by nearly half—with GDP per capita (purchasing power parity) falling from $3,900 in 2014 to $2,500 in 2016.[2] Furthermore, the war and the instability that preceded it have given such groups as AQAP and the Islamic State an opportunity to expand their influence throughout the country over time.

> More than two million have been displaced from their homes by the conflict, and GDP has fallen by nearly half.

This section explores the conflict and instability that have become part of daily life for the average Yemeni, with the goal of prefacing our later discussion of individual attitudes toward political violence in the midst of this conflict. We begin by providing a brief summary of Yemen's historical experience with conflict and instability, including three previous major civil wars, followed by a discussion of the political instability that preceded today's civil war, and then we summarize the key events of the current conflict. We also discuss the two major extremist elements currently operating in Yemen of interest to the U.S. counterterrorism community—AQAP and the Islamic State—as well as the sometimes-militant Southern Movement. We conclude by exploring what is known about the effect of this instability on the population studied in this research.

History of Conflict and Instability

In the past 50 years, Yemen has faced significant political instability, including multiple civil wars. From 1962 to 1970, an Egyptian-Saudi proxy war resulted in as many as 11,000 deaths, or about 0.3 percent of the entire population of Yemen's northern governorates where the fighting occurred. Given Yemen's population size of approximately 3.8 million at the time, the death toll from this lengthy conflict would be the equivalent of more than one million Americans dying in a civil war in 2016.[3] In later years, there was an 11-day failed coup d'état in 1986 in southern Yemen, in the then–People's Democratic Republic of Yemen. This brief coup killed some 13,000 Yemenis, equivalent to 0.6 percent of the entire population of Yemen's southern governorates.[4] Less than a decade later, as many as 7,000 additional Yemenis died in a 1994 civil war that pitted Yemen's newly unified southern and northern governorates against each other.[5]

Although Yemen was relatively stable politically from 1994 to 2011, the country continued to face significant pockets of subnational instability. This included persistent clashes (beginning as early as 1998) involving national security forces and tribal elements, particularly in the oil-rich governorate of Ma'rib, which reflected ongoing resistance by local tribes to state authority.[6] Beginning in 2004, this also included fighting with ethnic Houthi separatist elements along Yemen's border with Saudi Arabia, as well as the emergence of the separatist Southern Movement in 2007, which evolved from a nonviolent protest movement to a more violent movement by 2009.[7] Ultimately, this instability would include the rise of an al Qaeda franchise in Yemen, which enabled the 1998 attacks against U.S. embassies in Africa and executed the attack against the USS *Cole* in 2000. This al Qaeda franchise, as noted previously, would rise to notoriety as the most lethal al Qaeda affiliate based on U.S. estimates of potential threats to the homeland. Indeed, Yemen's historical instability, while "local," has frequently had global implications.

Yemen's Ongoing Civil War

Today's civil war has origins in 2011 and the Arab Spring. In the wake of the collapse of the government of Tunisia in 2011, Yemeni protesters took to the streets in major cities throughout Yemen to protest the reelection of then–President Ali Abdullah Saleh, who had been president since 1978.[8] After five months of protests that were frequently marred by violence and failed efforts by the Gulf Cooperation Council (GCC) to broker Saleh's resignation, Saleh was badly wounded in an attack on the presidential compound in June 2011 and traveled abroad for medical treatment.[9] Eight months later, after protracted negotiations by the GCC, the presidency was transitioned to Abd Rabbuh Mansur Hadi in February 2012, who was Saleh's vice president and acting president while Saleh was receiving medical treatment abroad.[10]

A key component of Yemen's transition agreement, which formalized Saleh's abdication, was the establishment of a National Dialogue Conference in Yemen as a two-year process that would lead to the formation of a new constitution and election of a new government.[11] The National Dialogue Conference concluded its negotiations in early 2014, and a new government was formed in November 2014 by then–President Hadi.[12] However, the Houthi movement, which had grown rapidly in strength and which by then controlled the capital city of Sana'a, opposed this government's formation.[13]

The influence of the northern-based Houthis expanded rapidly while the National Dialogue Conference was underway. The Houthis, who had fought several wars against President Saleh's forces beginning in 2004, had been largely contained in Yemen's most northern governorate of Sa'ada until the collapse of Saleh's government in 2011. But by late 2012, Houthi influence had expanded from its historic stronghold to neighboring provinces in northern Yemen.[14] And, in September 2014, following several weeks of Houthi-led protests against a cut in fuel subsidies, Houthi forces seized the capital after just four days of fighting.[15] Four months later, in January 2015, following the release of a new constitution opposed by the Houthis that divided Yemen into a federation of six regions with equal representation (with hopes of appeasing groups from the south), the Houthis seized the presidential compound and put Hadi under house arrest.[16] President Hadi fled to Aden the following month and declared Aden to be the capital of Yemen while the Houthis controlled Sana'a.[17]

On March 19, 2015, Houthi-affiliated forces assaulted Aden's international airport. Although this attack was repulsed by forces loyal to President Hadi, on March 21, the Sana'a–based Houthi leadership called for a "general mobilization of the military to confront 'terrorism'" in southern Yemen, and Houthi forces began to take control of major cities throughout Yemen's southern governorates.[18] On March 25, Hadi asked the United Nations (UN) Security Council "to back military action by 'willing countries' against the Houthi rebels," and Saudi airstrikes against Houthi positions commenced.[19] The civil war thus began.

With the onset of the civil war, Houthi forces began to rapidly expand their geographic sphere of influence.[20] The early Houthi expansion saw limited bloodshed, with Houthi forces facing very little resistance as they took control of major cities such as Taiz. By mid-2015, Houthis had either a presence or reported influence throughout most of Yemen.[21] This rapid expansion of Houthi control has been attributed to both support they received from former President Saleh, to whom many Yemeni army elements remained loyal, and Iranian backing, which the Houthis and Iran vigorously deny.[22]

This rapid expansion of Houthi control has been attributed to both support they received from former President Saleh . . . and to Iranian backing, which the Houthis and Iran vigorously deny.

Casualties in the civil war began to mount with the arrival of Arab coalition forces, led by Saudi Arabia, in support of the besieged but still internationally recognized President Hadi. The first month of operations—code named Operation Decisive Storm and involving aircraft from at least six Arab nations—left nearly 1,000 dead and 3,500 wounded in airstrikes throughout Houthi-controlled areas of Yemen.[23] After a month of airstrikes, which purportedly prevented the continued advance of Houthi forces but did little to push them back, the Arab coalition announced the beginning of Operation Restoring Hope, which would focus on finding a political solution in Yemen.[24] However, while Operation Restoring Hope called for an end to airstrikes, the air campaign against Houthi positions continued unabated.[25] The Hadi–Arab coalition began to make meaningful territorial gains against Houthi forces after Saudi and United Arab Emirates (UAE) ground forces deployed in support of President Hadi's beleaguered forces in Aden. This counteroffensive, Operation Golden Arrow, began to push Houthi forces from Yemen's southern governorates in July 2015.[26]

Despite the progress made by the coalition, Houthi forces remained in control of a vast amount of territory through early 2017, as shown in Figure 2.1. Areas in yellow indicate territory largely controlled by Houthi forces as of January 2017, including most of the western governorates of Yemen from Sa'ada in the north down through Sana'a and Taiz governorate in the south.

Intermittent calls by the UN for a truce and the beginning of peace talks over the course of the conflict have been marred by violence, with Arab coalition forces conducting airstrikes against Houthi positions within hours of a truce called for the Eid al-Fitr religious holiday in 2015.[27] Peace talks began again in earnest in April 2016, although these talks and a fragile truce have been threatened by continued airstrikes and accusations of Houthi violations of the ceasefire.[28] Continued efforts in 2016 to achieve a cessation of hostilities have similarly failed to achieve lasting peace.

Other Armed Groups in Yemen

In addition to the two primary antagonists in Yemen's civil war, a number of extremist and militant groups threaten Yemen's stability. This section reviews three of these elements: AQAP, the Islamic State, and the sometimes-militant Southern Movement. For each, we provide a brief background before summarizing their current role in the conflict.

Figure 2.1. Territorial Control by Armed Groups in Yemen as of January 2017

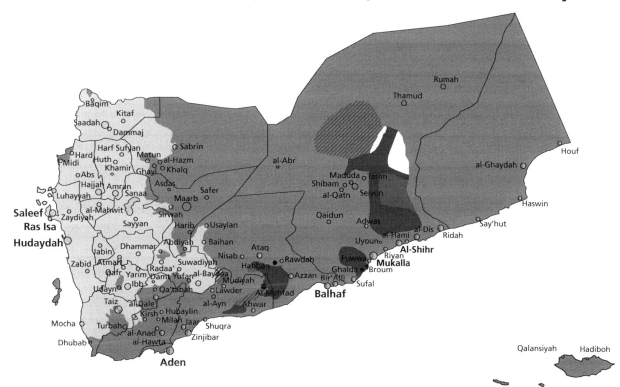

SOURCE: "#Yemen map: Conflict focus remains the south-west in #Taiz (#Dhubab), where coalition-backed troops try to retake areas near Bab al-Mandeb," Risk Intelligence on Twitter, January 17, 2017. Used with permission.
NOTES: Green areas represent territory controlled by or under the majority influence of government forces and their allies, popular resistance committees, and tribal allies. Blue dots represent the Southern Movement and Southern Resistance Committees (supported by the Arab coalition, comprising air cover with light presence of ground forces). Yellow areas represent territory controlled by former government, Houthi militants, and tribal allies. Gray areas represent territory controlled by or heavily influenced by AQAP (al Qaeda) and its tribal allies.
RAND RR1727-2.1

Al Qaeda in the Arabian Peninsula

AQAP emerged in early 2009 as a Yemen-based conglomeration of separate al Qaeda elements operating in Yemen and Saudi Arabia. While al Qaeda's previous manifestation in Yemen—which referred to itself as al Qaeda in Yemen—was involved in several domestic attacks, including a suicide attack against Spanish tourists and an attack against both the Italian and U.S. embassies,[29] the scale and scope of al Qaeda activities in Yemen expanded with the formation of AQAP. Indeed, within a few years of its formation, AQAP would claim responsibility for several attempted attacks against the United States, the publication of the English-language al Qaeda magazine *Inspire*, a variety of attacks against the Yemeni government,[30] and the attacks against the offices of *Charlie Hebdo* magazine in Paris in 2015.

At the onset of the current civil war, AQAP elements began to seize territory throughout southern governorates in Yemen. Al Mukalla, the capital of the governorate of Hadramawt and a major port city, was the first to be seized by

AQAP fighters in April 2015.[31] AQAP forces also would later capture Abyan governorate.[32] Although AQAP continued to control significant territory in southern Yemen by the time research was conducted for this report, UAE forces leading a force of more than 10,000 Yemeni fighters recaptured Al Mukalla from AQAP in April 2016.[33]

The Islamic State

In November 2014, the Islamic State announced the "expansion of the Islamic state" to multiple countries, including Yemen.[34] Many of these fighters in Yemen were defectors from AQAP. In March 2015, fighters affiliated with this Islamic State offshoot carried out a catastrophic attack in then-Houthi controlled Sana'a, killing nearly 140 worshippers at what has been described as pro-Houthi mosques.[35] Subsequently, Islamic State elements coordinated attacks against both the Houthis and forces loyal to Hadi, including car bombs and grisly executions filmed and disseminated as Islamic State propaganda.[36]

The Islamic State's strength in Yemen has been a source of debate. Some recent reporting suggests that the Islamic State has struggled to gain traction in Yemen, pointing to recent high-level defections from the organization.[37] Others have suggested that the Islamic State is gaining strength and "becoming just as dangerous as" AQAP.[38] An Islamic State attack against a military base in Aden in May 2016, which killed at least 45 army recruits, suggests that the threat from the Islamic State in Yemen should be taken seriously at least in terms of its lethality.[39]

Southern Movement

The Southern Movement, which formed in 2007 as a nonviolent effort to fight for increased political and economic opportunity for Yemen's southern governorates, evolved into a violent movement by 2009, reportedly in part because of harsh and mishandled responses from President Saleh's security forces.[40] After Hadi—himself from southern Yemen—assumed power in 2011, separatist violence from the Southern Movement subsided.[41] However, and despite the inclusion of representatives from the movement in the National Dialogue Conference, violence involving a "militant faction" of the Southern Movement erupted again in early 2013.[42]

In January 2015, following the seizure of the presidential palace and the forced resignation of President Hadi, elements from the Southern Movement who "outrightly rejected rule by the Houthis" seized checkpoints and government facilities in the southern governorates of Shabwa and Aden.[43] During Operation Decisive Storm, elements of the Southern Movement entered into a fragile alliance of convenience with the Hadi government to repel the Houthi militias from Aden.[44] But the alliance remains fragile. In February 2016, clashes erupted between presidential protection forces and Southern Movement militias in Aden.[45]

Effect of the Violence

Yemen today faces a humanitarian crisis as a result of the ongoing civil war. Beyond the more than 10,000 civilian casualties from the war, the civil war has left more than 8 percent of Yemen's population displaced from their homes.[46] Rates of internally displaced persons across Yemen are shown in Figure 2.2. More than 80 percent of the population require some form of humanitarian assistance after more than a year of conflict, including "14.4 million people unable to meet their food needs (of whom 7.6 million are severely food insecure), 19.4 million who lack clean water and sanitation (of whom 9.8 million lost access to water because of conflict), and 14.1 million without adequate healthcare."[47] Beyond the poverty, hunger, and poor health care—which disproportionately affected Yemen's children—the conflict has also damaged Yemen's "social fabric," with evidence that tribal, religious, and regional identities have eroded over the course of the war.[48]

Figure 2.2. Geography of Displaced Persons in Yemen

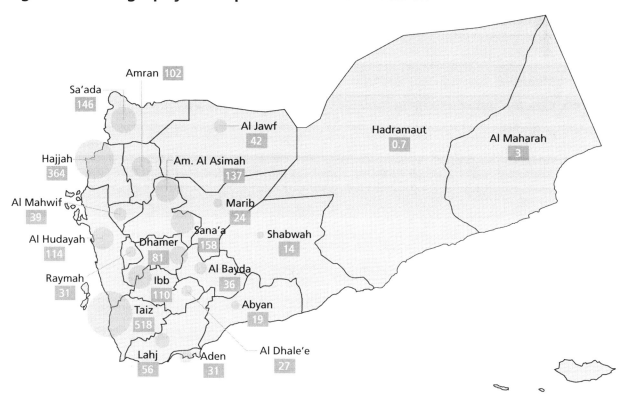

SOURCE: "Yemen: Humanitarian Snapshot—Overview on Population Movement," Humanitarian Response website, May 2016.
NOTE: Boxes indicate the number of internally displaced persons (in thousands) by governorate as of May 2016.
RAND *RR1727-2.2*

CHAPTER THREE

Methodology and Data

With Yemen's history of political violence now established, this chapter describes the conceptual framework of nonradicalization that underpins our research, as well as the methods and data used to examine nonradicalization in Yemen. Note that the appendix of this report provides more detail for those interested in the sampling methodology used in our research.

Conceptual Framework for Rejecting Violent Extremism

The methodological approach for this report begins with a conceptual framework for nonradicalization developed in prior iterations of this research. Our data collection and survey research were designed to capture the potential avenues of nonradicalization described in this framework. This framework (Figure 3.1) informed and shaped the questions asked of focus group and survey participants in Yemen. It was first derived from an extensive literature review of research related to the topic of why individuals reject violent extremism.[1]

As mentioned in the introduction, much of the CVE literature focuses on why individuals become involved in political violence. But it is not uncommon for researchers in the CVE field to report, for example, interviews with individuals who eventually choose not to engage in violence. Or, alternatively, researchers sometimes posit potential barriers to radicalization and willingness to engage in political violence. We used CVE research to build a conceptual framework for why some individuals choose, instead, to eschew violence. A full discussion of this literature can be found, as previously mentioned, in the first report of this series, "Resisting Violent Extremism."[2]

The methodological approach for this report begins with a conceptual framework for nonradicalization developed in prior iterations of this research.

In thinking about the conceptual framework (Figure 3.1), it helps to start at the top of the figure and work down. The framework suggests that, for membership in a terrorist group to decline, *new recruits do not join* and *existing members depart from the group*. In this report, as was true in the West Bank report, we focus on what predicts whether new recruits fail to join a terrorist group. Our literature-based framework posits that four overarching factors affect recruits' reluctance to join a terrorist group: (1) *moral repugnance* of violence, (2) the *perceived ineffectiveness of violence*, (3) the *perceived costs* of joining a group, and (4) an *absence of social ties* to influencers sympathetic to the terrorist group.

Continuing along the branches of this conceptual framework, on the left side of the figure, our second factor, *perceived ineffectiveness of violence*, has two sub-factors: *redirected pathways* and *apathy*. The framework posits that individuals will not participate in violence if either they believe that nonviolent avenues of political activity will be effective at achieving desired change or they are generally apathetic or believe that nothing at all will achieve desired change. Similarly, factor three, *perceived costs*, has three components: *fear of repression*,

Figure 3.1. Conceptual Framework

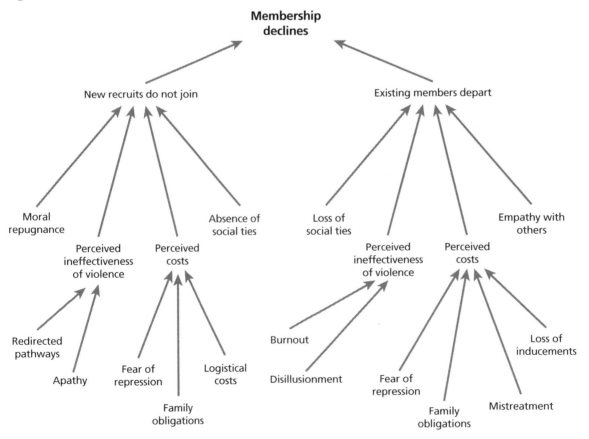

SOURCE: Cragin, 2013, p. 347.

RAND RR1727-3.1

family obligations, and the simple *logistical costs* of joining any given terrorist group.

Importantly, for those readers familiar with theories on individual radicalization, the pathways toward nonradicalization discussed in this framework are *not always* the exact opposite of the factors that lead individuals toward radicalization. Some are. For example, some consensus has emerged that individuals tend to radicalize in "peer groups," and our conceptual framework suggests that an absence of social ties is a factor contributing to nonradicalization.[3] But consider the two components of an individual's perceived ineffectiveness of violence—redirected pathways and apathy. These factors, which involve an individual's attitudes toward nonviolent mechanisms of achieving political change, do not simply capture the absence of radicalizing factors. Rather they acknowledge that nonviolent avenues toward political change can exist, even in the midst of radicalizing influencers. Indeed, the conceptual model used in this report presupposes that the motivations for rejecting violent extremism represent more than the simple dearth of motivations for radicalization. In other words, predictors of nonviolence are not simply the mirror opposites of those discussed for radicalization.[4]

Focus Groups

To assess the predictors of nonviolence in Yemen, our analysis draws first on a series of focus groups used to develop a better qualitative understanding of why individuals may choose not to engage in political violence in Yemen. As noted earlier, six focus groups were completed—four in Yemen's highly urban capital of Sana'a and two in rural districts outside of Sana'a. Of the six focus groups, three were male, three were female, and each group included men and women of varied educational backgrounds and ages. The focus groups aimed to explore key concepts in our survey in greater detail, such as political activity, prevalent social and religious organizations, and themes related to political, social, and religious change. Participants ranged in age from 18 to 34. Male participants included both employed and unemployed individuals, while female participants were predominantly housewives or students. Each focus group was administrated by local Yemeni partners with moderators who were fluent in local culture and language and came from the same ethnic group as the participants.[5]

A key component of the focus groups focused on understanding individual means of political activism and identifying how political views are formed and influenced. While many participants agreed that their political perspective is somewhat open to influence, participants also indicated that mistrust of the government and major political parties in Yemen made them cautious of being influenced by public figures at all or, at least, of admitting such influence. Many participants expressed dissatisfaction with and mistrust of the government, and, not surprisingly, many voiced a desire to affect change.

Interestingly, female participants identified social and religious organizations in Yemen as effective in generating positive change, while male participants identified the army and various militia groups as the key mechanisms through which political change is realized. While many participants suggested fair elections and better education could bring progress to Yemen, some condoned the use of boycotts, embargoes, or civil disobedience as ways to express their personal political beliefs. Across all groups involved in the focus groups, there was a consensus that change is needed in Yemen, that the political environment is highly volatile, and that current leaders do not prioritize the interests of the country or the public over their own personal interests.

Survey

Although significant survey work has been conducted in Yemen over the past decade, very little survey research has attempted to establish nationally representative findings.[6] Furthermore, while many of these surveys have focused on public health, education, and employment-related topics—and a smaller subset has examined Yemen's politics and stability—fewer still have focused on radicalization in Yemen. In designing our survey instrument, we attempted to integrate lessons learned from other survey efforts in Yemen with known best practices for survey research in conflict zones.

We used a cluster-based survey of 1,200 adults ages 18–64 in Yemen, collected by a partnered local survey firm. Fieldwork was conducted May 20–27, 2016, across Yemen in six governorates and the capital. This sample was designed to produce a national survey broadly (if not statistically) representative of the country as a whole, while accounting for variation in local conflict conditions. Our clustered sample includes respondents from six governorates and the capital, covering each of Yemen's six regions. Given periods of intense fighting in 2015 and proceeding through the time period in which fieldwork was conducted in early 2016, certain areas of the country were off limits to our survey team because of the risk to field personnel and survey respondents. In fact, during the fielding of our survey, enumerators in Hadramawt, Al Huday-dah, Ibb, and Ma'rib reported frequent or sporadic fighting within the two weeks prior to data collection. As a result, our sampling frame was selected in close consultation with local survey partners to produce a representative set of responses across a wide variety of socioeconomic, ethnic, and geographic areas, while maintaining minimal risk to field staff and respondents.

Figure 3.2 shows the six governorates, plus Sana'a, sampled in this survey. Blue stars indicate urban districts sampled in each governorate, while orange stars highlight rural districts. Notably, our sample included populations in Houthi-controlled territory as well as territory controlled by the Arab coalition. It also included populations in areas controlled or once controlled by AQAP and in proximity to Islamic State armed groups. These locations are indicated by the red dots in Figure 3.2.

Sample Design

Sampling was conducted in three enumeration areas (EAs) per governorate, across six governorates and Sana'a. EAs within each governorate were divided across one urban district (with one EA) and one rural district (with two EAs). Districts were randomly selected within each governorate. All EAs in Sana'a and Aden were urban. Table 3.1 shows the geographic distribution of our sample across Yemen by district, urban status, and sex. Sample sizes across districts and breakdowns by sex were allocated based on probability

Figure 3.2. Areas Sampled in National Survey

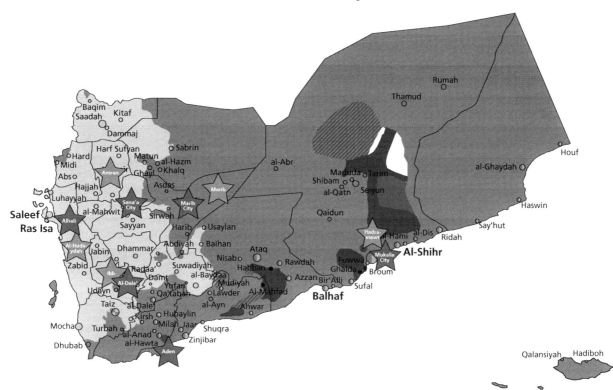

SOURCE: "#Yemen map: Conflict focus remains the south-west in #Taiz (#Dhubab), where coalition-backed troops try to retake areas near Bab al-Mandeb," Risk Intelligence on Twitter, January 17, 2017. Used with permission.
NOTES: Green areas represent territory controlled by or under the majority influence of government forces and their allies, popular resistance committees, and tribal allies. Blue dots represent the Southern Movement and Southern Resistance Committees (supported by the Arab coalition, comprising air cover with light presence of ground forces). Yellow areas represent territory controlled by former government, Houthi militants, and tribal allies. Gray areas represent territory controlled by or heavily influenced by AQAP (al Qaeda) and its tribal allies.
RAND RR1727-3.2

Table 3.1. Sampling Breakdown by Governorate, District, Urban Status, and Sex

GOVERNORATE	DISTRICT	URBAN STATUS	ENUMERATION AREAS	TOTAL SAMPLED	MALES SAMPLED	FEMALES SAMPLED
Sana'a	Shuoob	Urban	3	205	111	94
Ibb	Aldahr	Urban	1	39	20	19
	Ibb	Rural	2	193	94	99
Al Hudaydah	Alhali	Urban	1	75	40	35
	Aldurihmi	Rural	2	158	82	76
Hadramawt	Mukalla city	Urban	1	76	41	35
	Mukalla	Rural	2	80	41	39
Aden	Almansoura	Urban	3	126	68	58
Ma'rib	Ma'rib city	Urban	1	14	8	6
	Ma'rib	Rural	2	88	46	42
Amran	Amran	Urban	1	27	14	13
	Eyal Sorih	Rural	2	119	61	58
Total			21	1,200	626	574

proportional to size sampling, producing a self-weighted sample.

Based on our clustered sample design, we needed to account for the fact that individuals in the same EA exhibited some amount of dependence or similarity when measuring the statistical power of our sample. This similarity reduces precision and power relative to a simple random sample of the same sample size that does not collect data in clusters. We estimate intracluster correlations using a variety of key variables in our survey, and calculate an expected *margin of error* (ME) for findings from our study of between 2 and 7 percent.[7] Further, we expected to reliably measure minimum detectable odds ratios (ORs) that range from 2.01 to 5.59.

Using existing microdata from prior survey research in Yemen, we can assess the extent to which our sample is comparable to other areas of Yemen in terms of socioeconomic traits. Table 3.2 presents descriptive statistics comparing demographic breakdowns from our sample relative to national averages measured in the 2004 Yemeni Census.[8]

As shown in the table, there are modest differences in the distribution of respondents by sex and age in our sample relative to their national averages. Major differences exist in the level of education of our sample relative to national averages from the 2004 census. Whereas 66 percent of our sample has a primary education or higher, national estimates suggest that only 23 percent of the entire country possesses this level of education. Some of this is based solely on the areas included in our sample—levels of illiteracy in our

Table 3.2. Demographic Comparison with 2004 Census

DEMOGRAPHICS		2016 SURVEY (%)	2004 CENSUS (%)
Sex	Male	52.6	51.0
	Female	47.4	49.0
Education	Illiterate or read and write	33.5	76.7
	Primary to diploma	30.1	13.0
	Bachelor's or higher	36.4	10.2
Age	18–34	51.0	56.5
	35–64	49.0	43.5

SOURCE: Authors' estimates and Central Statistical Organization—Ministry of Planning and International Cooperation, 2004.

sampled districts are lower than nonsampled districts based on the same 2004 census data. Furthermore, it is logical to assume that communities in more remote and underdeveloped areas of Yemen would exhibit a greater hesitance toward participating because of a lack of prior exposure to similar survey research. Finally, demographic shifts since the 2004 census have contributed to a Yemen that is largely younger in age and likely more educated as well. We believe our sample captures sufficient variation in demographic traits across Yemen and is largely representative of the Yemeni population, particularly given the limitations of conducting survey research in a conflict zone.[9]

Demographic characteristics aside, it is also important to cast the areas sampled in light of the greater conflict in Yemen described earlier in this report. As discussed previously, our sample covers Houthi-dominant areas in and around Sana'a, Al Hudaydah, Ibb, and Amran, as well as AQAP hotspots, including Al Mukalla (in Hadramawt) and Aden. Both Al Mukalla and Aden also have experienced conflict that involved security forces from the UAE and the Arab coalition. In general, we believe our sample includes a mix of individuals subject to potential radicalization by antigovernment forces more generally, as well as those exposed to foreign actors seeking to influence the outcome of the civil war and those who are subject to the influence of radical jihadists.

Dependent Variables: Descriptive Statistics

This report focuses on two measures of nonradicalization as dependent variables: (1) individuals' opposition toward political violence in general and (2) their personal choice not to engage in political violence. This is an important distinction. Although both measure individuals' "openness" to political violence, not everyone who refrains from violent acts opposes violence in principle. Focusing on this distinction builds on our prior research in the West Bank, which found a clear difference between support for suicide bomb-

It is logical to assume that communities in more remote and underdeveloped areas of Yemen would exhibit a greater hesitance toward participating because of a lack of prior exposure to similar survey research.

ings in theory and willingness to actually engage in violent protests personally.

Opposition Toward Political Violence

To further understand opposition toward political violence in general, we asked a series of questions in our survey related to each respondent's level of support or opposition to (1) a friend who travels abroad to conduct attacks against a foreign occupier, (2) a friend who travels abroad to conduct attacks against Muslim governments, (3) attacks against foreigners, including aid workers, within Yemen, and (4) attacks conducted inside Yemen against Yemeni civilians. Table 3.3 shows the overarching results from these questions.

For this study, we focused primarily on opposition to attacks abroad against foreign occupiers for two reasons. First, calls to conduct such attacks are frequent among radicalizing elements throughout Yemen, particularly AQAP, but have also been made by the Houthi rebels, who often use the slogan, "Death to America, death to Israel."[10] And, second, we found that most respondents largely felt that violence inside Yemen's borders against civilians of any nationality was unjustified. Notably, respondents actually felt that attacks against Yemeni civilians were more justifiable than attacks against foreign civilians inside Yemen. This points to a key finding of this report: Yemenis appear to conflate violence with political activism in this instance, particularly in the context of a bloody civil war that has claimed thousands of Yemeni civilians' lives. In fact, attitudes toward domestic attacks against Yemeni civilians appear to be driven largely by conflict conditions in the ongoing civil war.[11]

Importantly, we asked respondents to characterize their own willingness to

Table 3.3. Opposition Toward Political Violence

SURVEY QUESTIONS	GREAT EXTENT	MEDIUM EXTENT	LIMITED EXTENT	NOT AT ALL
To what extent is it justified for a group or individual to launch an armed attack against Yemeni civilians?	2.1%	10.3%	8%	79.6%
To what extent is it justified for a group or individual to launch an armed attack against foreigners, including aid workers?	1.5%	1.6%	5.7%	91.2%

SURVEY QUESTIONS	STRONGLY AGREE	SOMEWHAT AGREE	SOMEWHAT DISAGREE	STRONGLY DISAGREE
Do you support a friend traveling abroad to assist Muslims fighting their own government?	17.8%	8.3%	11.8%	62.1%
Do you support a friend traveling abroad to assist Muslims fighting a foreign occupier?	52.9%	22.1%	5%	19.9%

support a friend traveling overseas to fight—rather than whether they were willing to travel themselves—because of the sensitivity of the topic. That is, we expected that respondents would be more willing to answer a question related to their friends' violent activity or beliefs as a proxy for their own responses in an effort to diminish social undesirability. Table 3.4 shows the frequency of support and opposition to this first measure of nonradicalization across Yemen in our survey.

One-quarter of all respondents across Yemen disagree or strongly disagree that they would support a friend traveling abroad to fight against foreign forces occupying Muslim lands. Notably, a large percentage of respondents in Aden, Al Hudaydah, and Ma'rib supports travel to fight a foreign occupier, while noteworthy minorities of individuals in Amran, Hadramawt, Ibb, and Sana'a express their opposition to such support. This geographic roster does not fall neatly within one social cleavage of Yemen: Ma'rib's hyper-tribal society stands in contrast to Al Hudaydah's ethnic diversity, and the agrarian economies of both contrast with Aden's urbanization. Nor does support for a friend's travel to fight a foreign occupier concentrate in a specific region frequented by one armed group over another.

Personal Choice to Not Engage in Political Violence

To measure an individual's choice to not engage in violence, we asked a series of questions related to violent and nonviolent protests. This addresses the more immediate issue of nonradicalization: Beyond an individual's theoretical attitudes toward political violence, can we explain why some individuals choose not to actually engage in violence themselves? As discussed earlier, violent protests were a common occurrence in the run-up to President Saleh's abdication in 2011. Many of these protests started as street demonstrations that turned violent in clashes with security forces. More generally, the concept of a violent protest is familiar to many Yemenis as a form of political protest:

Table 3.4. Do You Support a Friend Traveling Abroad to Fight a Foreign Occupier?

GOVERNORATE	STRONGLY AGREE (%)	AGREE (%)	DISAGREE (%)	STRONGLY DISAGREE (%)
Whole sample	52.9	22.1	5.0	19.9
Aden	87.1	11.3	1.6	0.0
Amran	23.4	37.9	9.7	29.0
Hadramawt	42.2	17.5	3.9	36.4
Al Hudaydah	69.9	24.0	2.2	3.9
Ibb	46.4	11.6	5.4	36.6
Ma'rib	58.2	30.8	4.4	6.6
Sana'a	46.8	26.6	7.9	18.7

Focus-group participants expressed a familiarity with street demonstrations and violence when describing their own views toward political activism.

Despite this familiarity, however, almost all respondents expressed an unwillingness to participate in such protests themselves (98.6 percent) (Table 3.5). The table also shows the regional breakdown of our results across these measures.

Respondents did indicate that their family and friends were more willing to engage in violent protests than they were themselves. Based partly on discussions with our survey field team, we believe that responses to questions regarding family or friends' willingness to engage in violence also capture each individual's personal choice to engage in violence, given the sensitivity of the question. Combining these measures, we found that 91 percent of respondents stated that neither they themselves nor their friends or family were likely to engage in violent protests. This combined indicator represents our second dependent variable, capturing the actual choice to engage in violence.

Independent Variables: Descriptive Statistics

This section details the main independent variables used to assess predictors of nonradicalization, as outlined in our conceptual framework. It also provides descriptive statistics summarizing responses to these specific survey questions.

Perceived Ineffectiveness of Violence

Our conceptual framework for nonradicalization offers two potential factors that could contribute to a perception that violence is not the most effective means of achieving political change: (1) redirected pathways or a belief that

Table 3.5. Choice to Engage in Violence: Willingness to Participate in Violent Protests

	UNLIKELY OR VERY UNLIKELY TO ENGAGE IN VIOLENT PROTESTS			
GOVERNORATE	SELF (%)	FAMILY (%)	FRIENDS (%)	COMBINED (%)
Whole sample	98.6	96.8	95.2	91.5
Aden	99.2	100.0	97.6	96.7
Amran	99.3	99.3	97.7	96.9
Hadramawt	100.0	90.4	99.3	89.5
Al Hudaydah	98.3	97.8	99.1	95.6
Ibb	99.6	100.0	97.0	96.5
Ma'rib	97.7	98.7	85.0	83.3
Sana'a	96.5	92.1	85.2	78.4

nonviolent political activity is likely to be effective at achieving progress and (2) apathy, or a belief that no level of activism—violent or not—will achieve change in society.

To measure these factors, the survey asked a series of questions to gauge the extent to which respondents were politically active, including: (1) Are you a member of a political or social organization? (2) How often do you discuss politics with others in your free time? and (3) Are you very, fairly, somewhat, or not at all politically active? It also asked a series of questions about each respondent's attitudes toward the pace of political, social, or economic change and their overall outlook for future life in Yemen.[12] We focus on three variables specifically to capture redirected pathways and apathy—the level of political activity of each respondent, respondents' endorsement of the notion that "no matter how hard we try, nothing in this country changes," and their outlook that their own lives will be better than their parents' lives. Table 3.6 presents descriptive statistics on respondents' answers to these questions.

Although only 7.4 percent of respondents stated that they were very or fairly political active, respondents in two governorates exhibited well above average levels of political activity—Ma'rib and Sana'a, at 20 percent and 19 percent, respectively. One possible explanation for these outliers is that the physical security buffer provided by Houthi forces and Arab coalition forces in these two governorates provides inhabitants with an opportunity to participate in politics without fear of reprisal from rival groups. In terms of individual apathy and attitudes toward change in Yemen, across all regions, respondents expressed consistent optimism that their lives would be better than those of their parents, at a rate of 72.5 percent across all regions, urban and rural.

Table 3.6. Distribution of Responses Measuring Perceived Ineffectiveness of Violence

INDEPENDENT VARIABLE	SAMPLE AVERAGE (%)	RANGE ACROSS GOVERNORATES (%)
Level of political activity	7.4 Very or fairly active	0.60–20.0
	92.5 Not very or not at all active	80.0–99.3
No matter how hard we try, nothing in this country changes	49.5 Agree or strongly agree	36.4–62.2
	50.4 Disagree or strongly disagree	28.8–63.6
Belief that life will be better than own parents'	72.5 Very or fairly optimistic	62.4–80.9
	27.6 Very or fairly pessimistic	19.1–37.6

Endorsement of the belief that "no matter how hard we try, nothing in this country changes," varied heavily by governorate, with Ibb governorate showing the largest sense of disaffection with political progress, and Hadramawt showing the least disaffection.

Perceived Costs of Violence

To better understand the perceived costs of violence for Yemenis in our sample, the survey asked a series of questions about respondents' attitudes toward their own safety, as well as the safety of family members and friends. Table 3.7 presents the distribution of survey responses for these independent variables. The first row in Table 3.7 reports answers to a single question: How concerned are you about being assaulted in the future? Surprisingly, most Yemenis in our sample suggested they had little to no concern that they would be assaulted by armed groups in the future. Across the sample, only 27.2 percent of respondents were somewhat or very concerned about being assaulted; respondents sampled in Aden reported significantly more fear of assault by security forces (64.3 percent) than respondents in other parts of the country.

Table 3.7. Distribution of Responses Measuring Perceived Costs of Violence

INDEPENDENT VARIABLE	SAMPLE AVERAGE (%)	RANGE ACROSS GOVERNORATES (%)
Concern over future assault by armed groups	27.2 Very or somewhat concerned	0.6–64.3
	72.8 A little or not at all concerned	35.7–99.4
Past assaults by security forces	1.0 Personally assaulted	0–2.4
	5.3 Family assaulted	0.6–14.6
	9.6 Friend assaulted	0–21.4
Past retaliation by rival group	4.0 Personally retaliated against	0–7.8
	10.8 Friend retaliated against	0–20.7
	10.6 Friend retaliated against	0–46.8
Past retaliation by own group	3.1 Personally retaliated against	0–9.9
	5.1 Family retaliated against	0–12.2
	6.8 Friend retaliated against	0–14.1

At the other end of the scale, those in Hadramawt and Ibb reported being the least concerned about future assault.

The second row in Table 3.7 reports whether respondents themselves, family members, or friends have ever been assaulted by security forces or retaliated against by rival groups or their own groups in the past. As before, we see respondents consistently underreport their own histories of retaliation, relative to the rates at which their family and friends have been assaulted by security forces or retaliated against by a rival group or their own group.

Social Ties

For the next pathway through which nonradicalization may occur in our conceptual framework, respondents were asked to articulate the extent to which their parents, friends, or religious leaders had influence over their major life decisions. We asked this series of questions to better understand the roles that social ties play in strengthening attitudes toward political violence in Yemen. Respondents largely stated that outside influencers (including parents, friends, and imams) had little effect on their major life decisions. We believe that this lower-than-expected level of influence and minimal level of social connectivity correspond with the general distrust of political and social leaders in Yemen, as revealed in our focus groups. Table 3.8 shows results from these survey questions.

Religiosity and Religious Conservatism

Finally, although religiosity and religious conservatism do not play a central role in our conceptual framework for nonradicalization, we did ask a series of questions to better understand the effect of this variable on attitudes toward

Table 3.8. Distribution of Responses Measuring Social Ties

INDEPENDENT VARIABLE	SAMPLE AVERAGE (%)	RANGE ACROSS GOVERNORATES (%)
Parents' influence on major decisions	67.2 Great or fair amount	52.8–74.0
	32.9 Only a little or none	25.9–47.3
Friends' influence on major decisions	33.0 Great or fair amount	21.3–45.2
	67.0 Only a little or none	62.7–78.7
Imams' influence on major decisions	22.7 Great or fair amount	3.2–31.0
	77.3 Only a little or none	69.1–96.8

Support for educating boys and girls in the same classroom, a conventionally taboo social issue for conservative Muslims, was endorsed by 43.9 percent of respondents.

political violence in Yemen given its salience in the larger CVE literature. The influence of extreme religious views is often used as an explanation for radicalization, and so we sought to gauge the importance of "moderate" religious views on opposition to political violence. To do this, we asked respondents whether, generally speaking, they would describe themselves as very, somewhat, or not at all religious. We also asked a series of questions about religious practices and socioreligious beliefs; these included individuals' attitudes toward the following statements: (1) Non-Muslims should have the same rights as Muslims; (2) religious practices are private and should be kept separate from social, political, and economic life; and (3) boys and girls can be educated in the same classroom. In Table 3.9, we present descriptive statistics about religiosity and focus on one specific measure of religious conservatism, the social acceptability of cogendered education.

Although religious and cultural attitudes varied heavily with regard to social conservatism, the vast majority of respondents (92.7 percent) across the sample indicated that they are *religious or somewhat religious*. This high level of religiosity, however, did not correlate directly with support for traditionally conservative social values. Support for educating boys and girls in the same classroom, a conventionally taboo social issue for conservative Muslims, was endorsed by 43.9 percent of respondents. Aden and Al Hudaydah expressed the lowest rates of religious conservatism based on cogendered education, with a belief that gender-integrated classrooms were permissible among 71.5 percent and 60.1 percent of respondents, respectively. The difference between religiosity and religious conservatism in Yemen has interesting implications for measuring political attitudes and radicalization, because it suggests that participation in religious and social institutions may not always translate directly into conservative religious beliefs.

Table 3.9. Distribution of Responses Measuring Religiosity and Religious Conservatism

INDEPENDENT VARIABLE	SAMPLE AVERAGE (%)	RANGE ACROSS GOVERNORATES (%)
How religious are you?	92.7 Religious or somewhat religious	84.9–99.3
	7.30 Not religious	0.60–13.0
Boys and girls can be educated in the same classroom	43.9 Strongly agree or agree	19.6–71.5
	56.1 Strongly disagree or disagree	28.6–80.4

CHAPTER FOUR

Results

This chapter presents the results of our empirical examination of nonradicalization in Yemen using the dependent variables and independent variables laid out in the previous chapter. It begins by discussing the empirical model and follows with a discussion of the results of logistic regressions on each of our two dependent variables measuring attitudes toward political violence.

Empirical Model

As established in Chapter Three, we use two distinct measures of nonradicalization: (1) opposition to travel abroad to fight a foreign occupier (as a measure of individual opposition to political violence in general) and (2) unwillingness to engage in violent protests (as a measure of the personal choice not to engage in violence). Although asked on a Likert-like scale in our survey, we dichotomized each dependent variable and conduct logistic regressions to model the predictors of nonradicalization in each case. The following equation offers our empirical approach.

$$DV_i^{(0,1)} = B_0 + B_1 X_i + B_2 X_{gov} + \varepsilon_q.$$

Respondent i's attitudes toward political violence, $DV_i^{(0,1)}$, are modeled as a function of some constant B_0 and by a vector of covariates X_i and governorate-level fixed effects X_{gov}, and an error term ε_q, which is clustered by sampling enumeration area q.

Two logistic regressions are computed, one for each dependent variable across the entire vector of covariates X_i and X_{gov}.[1] We present the results of these regressions in the subsequent sections. The results have been broken into sections of similar covariates based on our conceptual framework for ease of discussion. Each table in this section therefore represents a portion of the results of the two larger logistic regressions across all covariates and should not be interpreted as individual regressions run only on each subset of covariates. Combined regression tables showing the results seen in this chapter, but organized in a traditional tabular roster of all regression coefficients, are presented in the appendix.

Individuals in Yemen appear to conflate political violence with political activism.

Perceived Ineffectiveness of Violence

Our conceptual framework focuses on two different factors that may drive individuals to believe that violence is not the most effective means of achieving political change: redirected pathways and apathy. We explored the effect of these drivers on our dependent variables using data on respondents' level of political activity, their overall view toward life in Yemen relative to that of their parents' generation, and attitudes toward the hope of political, social or economic change. The results are shown in Table 4.1. These estimates control for the full set of covariates presented throughout this chapter, although only marginal effects related to the perceived ineffectiveness of violence are presented in this table.

Our model reveals that politically active individuals are *less likely* to oppose overseas travel by a friend to fight against foreign occupiers and less likely to be unwilling to engage in violence. That is, political activism does not appear to contribute to individuals rejecting violent extremism in either form; in fact, it arguably increases radicalization. Individuals in Yemen appear to conflate political violence with political activism.

Similarly, we also find that individuals who are optimistic about their own life relative to prior generations are marginally less willing to engage (or have

Table 4.1. Perceived Ineffectiveness of Violence

	DOES NOT SUPPORT TRAVEL ABROAD TO FIGHT FOREIGN OCCUPIER	UNWILLING TO ENGAGE IN VIOLENT PROTESTS
Very or fairly politically active	−0.219***	−0.036**
	(0.063)	(0.018)
Very or fairly optimistic life will be better than parents	0.004	0.031*
	(0.034)	(0.017)
No matter how hard we try, nothing in this country changes	−0.014	−0.002
	(0.031)	(0.020)

NOTES: Marginal effects of a logistic regression are presented, with standard errors clustered by EA presented in parentheses. Statistical significance is denoted by * $p < 0.1$, ** $p < 0.05$, *** $p < 0.01$. Regression results presented in this table control for the full array of covariates presented in our combined model, shown throughout this chapter as well as in the statistical appendix.

family or friends who engage) in violent protests. By comparison, apathetic feelings toward the hope of progress in Yemen are insignificant in both the choice to engage in violence and opposition to violence in theory.

Perceived Costs of Violence

Our conceptual model also includes fear of repression as a possible factor in mitigating support for political violence. Overall, the results suggest (as shown in Table 4.2) that an individual's concern over future assault has little effect on their opposition to violence in theory; it also has little effect on their choice to engage in violent protests. Similarly, past assault by security forces against a respondent or their family has no statistically significant effect on

Table 4.2. Perceived Costs of Violence

	DOES NOT SUPPORT TRAVEL ABROAD TO FIGHT FOREIGN OCCUPIER	UNWILLING TO ENGAGE IN VIOLENT PROTESTS
Very or somewhat concerned about future assault	0.036	0.009
	(0.036)	(0.021)
Self—assaulted by security forces in past	0.114	0.024
	(0.089)	(0.119)
Family—assaulted by security forces in past	−0.074	−0.038
	(0.064)	(0.042)
Friend—assaulted by security forces in past	0.080*	−0.075**
	(0.047)	(0.038)
Self—retaliated against by rival group in past	0.014	0.007
	(0.054)	(0.028)
Family—retaliated against by rival group in past	0.094*	0.027
	(0.052)	(0.038)
Friend—retaliated against by rival group in past	−0.204	−0.019
	(0.149)	(0.048)
Self—retaliated against by own group in past	−0.160*	0.000
	(0.097)	(0.058)
Family—retaliated against by own group in past	0.034	−0.054
	(0.075)	(0.073)
Friend—retaliated against by own group in past	0.023	0.060*
	(0.116)	(0.032)
Frequent or sporadic fighting in last two weeks	0.005	0.095*
	(0.102)	(0.052)

NOTES: Marginal effects of a logistic regression are presented, with standard errors clustered by EA presented in parentheses. Statistical significance is denoted by * $p < 0.1$ and ** $p < 0.05$. Regression results presented in this table control for the full array of covariates presented in our combined model, shown throughout this chapter as well as in the statistical appendix.

either dependent variable. Respondents whose friends have been assaulted by security forces appear more likely to engage in violence, but marginally less likely to support it in theory.

Past retaliation by rival groups appears to have little to do with respondents' choice to engage in violence or support it in theory—except that respondents' whose families were retaliated against by a rival group are marginally more likely to condemn political violence in theory. Retaliation against the respondent by their own group appears to lead them to support violence overseas, but marginally less likely to engage in violence at home.

These nuanced results point to an interesting narrative detailing the effect that fear of repression has on Yemeni civilians today in the midst of a persistent civil war. Specifically, assaults by security forces may drive individuals (on the margins) toward violence locally as a form of immediate revenge. At the same time, some factors related to the fear of repression appear to disincentivize support for violence overseas more generally, perhaps as individuals internalize these high costs of violence. Affirming this point, respondents in districts where there was frequent or sporadic fighting within the last two weeks were marginally more likely to not engage in violent protests.

Social Ties

To better understand the effect of strong social ties between respondents and their parents, friends, and imams, we distinguish between three types of social influencers—parents, friends, and imams. Results are shown in Table 4.3. Strong social ties between respondents and these three types of influencers appear to have no clear direction of effect on the choice to actually engage in violent protests across our sample. However, they greatly affect an individual's attitudes toward political violence in theory. Specifically, respondents whose parents and friends exert a great or fair amount of influence on their major life decisions are significantly less likely to oppose a friend's travel abroad to fight a foreign occupier. These findings affirm that there is an attitudinal difference between predictors of support for political violence in theory and personal willingness to engage in violence. Treating these two forms of nonradicalization as distinct is important for designing effective CVE programs.

Notably, respondents who are greatly influenced by imams are no more or less likely to endorse political violence in theory or practice. Given the disaffection among participants in our focus groups for more traditional authority figures in Yemen, these respondents may be affected by this general skepticism toward formal influencers outside of family and friends.

Table 4.3. Social Ties

	DOES NOT SUPPORT TRAVEL ABROAD TO FIGHT FOREIGN OCCUPIER	UNWILLING TO ENGAGE IN VIOLENT PROTESTS
Parents have great or fair amount of influence	−0.061**	0.010
	(0.029)	(0.028)
Friends have great or fair amount of influence	−0.102***	0.013
	(0.023)	(0.028)
Imams have great or fair amount of influence	−0.016	−0.012
	(0.041)	(0.018)

Note: Marginal effects of a logistic regression are presented, with standard errors clustered by EA presented in parentheses. Statistical significance is denoted by ** $p < 0.05$ and *** $p < 0.01$. Regression results presented in this table control for the full array of covariates presented in our combined model, shown throughout this chapter as well as in the statistical appendix.

Religiosity and Demographic Traits

We next examine whether religiosity, religious conservatism, and demographic traits such as sex, education, age, and employment status affect individual nonradicalization in Yemen. Results are shown in Table 4.4. Across different levels of religiosity, respondents show few differences in their opposition to political violence in theory or in practice. In terms of respondents' religious conservatism, our results suggest that those with more moderate religious views are more likely to oppose attacks against foreign occupiers abroad: Specifically, those who believe it is acceptable for boys and girls to be educated in the same classroom are significantly more likely to oppose such violence.

We also include a standard set of demographic covariates in our model, including sex, education, age, and employment status. Descriptive statistics for each of these demographic variables were presented in an earlier section, with the exception of employment status. We note then that 43 percent of respondents in our sample were employed full-time, part-time, or as a daily low-wage laborer; 14 percent were unemployed; and 43 percent were out of the labor force.

Adding all of these variables into our empirical models presented in Table 4.4 reveals that men are marginally more likely to oppose fighting a foreign occupier than women, but they show few differences with women in terms of the choice to actually engage in violence. And, while increased education is often cited as a pathway through which individuals can reject violent extremism, we find no evidence that individuals with higher levels of education behave differently in terms of their attitudes toward nonviolence or willingness to engage in violence. We do find that individuals who are

Those who believe it is acceptable for boys and girls to be educated in the same classroom are significantly more likely to oppose such violence.

Table 4.4. Religiosity and Demographic Traits

	DOES NOT SUPPORT FOREIGN TRAVEL TO FIGHT OCCUPIER	UNWILLING TO ENGAGE IN VIOLENT PROTESTS
Religious or somewhat religious (versus not religious)	0.018	−0.010
	(0.078)	(0.019)
Boys and girls can be educated in same classroom	0.076**	0.017
	(0.034)	(0.014)
Male (versus female)	0.184**	0.009
	(0.073)	(0.030)
Primary to diploma (versus illiterate or read/write)	0.005	0.009
	(0.051)	(0.027)
BA or higher (versus illiterate or read/write)	0.043	0.006
	(0.054)	(0.022)
Full-time, part-time employed or wage laborer (versus out of the labor force)	−0.084**	−0.016
	(0.042)	(0.024)
Unemployed (versus out of labor force)	−0.058*	0.012
	(0.035)	(0.024)
Age 35–64 (versus age 18–34)	0.047	0.022
	(0.032)	(0.018)

Note: Marginal effects of a logistic regression are presented, with standard errors clustered by EA presented in parentheses. Statistical significance is denoted by * $p < 0.1$ and ** $p < 0.05$. Regression results presented in this table control for the full array of covariates presented in our combined model, shown throughout this chapter as well as in the statistical appendix.

employed are significantly more likely to support fighting a foreign occupier abroad than those who are out of the labor force. We find marginal differences in the same direction between unemployed individuals and those who are out of the labor force, suggesting that those who have an economic interest in achieving political change are more likely to embrace violence to achieve that change. We find no differences between older and younger individuals in terms of their decision to engage in violence or support travel abroad by a friend to fight.

Geographic Variation

Finally, we show in Table 4.5 estimates of governorate fixed effects and covariates unique to the locations sampled in this study, including whether each respondent lives in an urban or rural district. We find that urban residents are significantly more willing to engage in violence, but that they are significantly less likely to support a friend traveling to fight a foreign occupier abroad. We also see that respondents in Sana'a, Al Hudaydah, Aden, and Ma'rib show significant tendencies on average toward support for political violence abroad relative to the largely stable Ibb governorate.

Table 4.5. Geographic Variation

	DOES NOT SUPPORT FOREIGN TRAVEL TO FIGHT OCCUPIER	UNWILLING TO ENGAGE IN VIOLENT PROTESTS
Urban District	0.117**	−0.091***
	(0.052)	(0.028)
Ibb	*Reference*	*Reference*
Sana'a	−0.301***	−0.040*
	(0.084)	(0.022)
Al Hudaydah	−0.469***	−0.100
	(0.113)	(0.075)
Hadramawt	−0.152	−0.158*
	(0.155)	(0.094)
Aden	−0.516***	0.023
	(0.091)	(0.021)
Ma'rib	−0.182	−0.079
	(0.212)	(0.149)
Amran	−0.100	0.032
	(0.113)	(0.023)

Note: Marginal effects of a logistic regression are presented, with standard errors clustered by EA presented in parentheses. Statistical significance is denoted by * $p < 0.1$, ** $p < 0.05$, *** $p < 0.01$. Regression results presented in this table control for the full array of covariates presented in our combined model, shown throughout this chapter.

Chapter Five delves into the policy implications of these results for better understanding nonradicalization in Yemen. We want to caution readers, at this point, from overgeneralizing the findings of these analyses, which must first be taken in the unique context of Yemen's ongoing civil war.

Taiz City, Yemen

Findings and Implications

What motivates individuals to engage in political violence at home or abroad? It is easy to posit answers to this question in theory—political disenfranchisement, lack of economic opportunities, and extremist ideologies are frequently cited as radicalizing factors. But in truth, the actual drivers of political violence are not so simple. And there is still so much that we do not know. Nonetheless, tangible answers to these questions are essential for U.S. government officials, civil society groups, and activists as they attempt to formulate effective policies and implement programs to undermine violent extremism.

This report attempts to fill this gap in knowledge. It represents the third in a series of papers devoted to the topic of nonradicalization.[1] The first, "Rejecting Violent Extremism," presented a conceptual framework of nonradicalization. The second explored this framework through semistructured interviews and a survey in the Palestinian West Bank. This third report continues this research by examining why individuals reject violence in Yemen, through survey and focus group research. It argues that the best way to undermine violent extremism is to strengthen those factors that motivate individuals to reject political violence. What are those factors as they relate to Yemen? How can policymakers strengthen nonradicalization? This chapter addresses the policy implications of five key findings, summarized as follows.

> The best way to undermine violent extremism is to strengthen those factors that motivate individuals to reject political violence.

Key Findings

- Choosing not to engage in violence is *attitudinally distinct* from opposing political violence in theory.

- Urban centers represent important populations for strengthening nonradicalization.

- Yemenis perceive attacks against local civilians as more legitimate than attacks against foreigners, including aid workers.

- Social ties, measured by the degree of influence exerted by family, friends, and religious leaders, also do not affect individual radicalization in one clear direction.

- Yemenis view political violence as a form of activism, so redirected pathways—or participation in nonviolent activism—do not diminish a propensity for violence.

Policy Implications

The first key finding is that choosing not to engage in violence is *attitudinally distinct* from opposing political violence in theory. To arrive at this finding, the survey asked respondents a series of questions to delineate (1) individuals who were unlikely to engage in violence and (2) those who opposed political violence in theory. The results suggest that very real distinctions exist between predictors of each form of nonradicalization, and that strengthening opposition to violence in theory is different from strengthening opposition to violence in practice.

Perhaps the most striking result showing a difference between support for violence in theory and practice had to do with the effect of strong social ties. Results suggested that respondents whose family and friends had significant influence over their decisions were significantly less likely to oppose political violence in theory. However, these strong social ties had no clear influence on an individual's choice to engage in political violence at home. We found a similar difference when looking at the effect of religious conservatism. Those individuals who opposed political violence in theory were more likely to agree that it is acceptable for boys and girls to be educated in the same classroom. That is, individuals who opposed violence in theory were *not* religiously conservative. However, religious conservatism had little to do with individual attitudes toward physically engaging in political violence.

This finding is more than academic; it has larger implications for U.S. policy in Yemen. Logically, if choosing not to engage in violence is distinct from opposing violence in theory, then interventions that treat both forms of nonradicalization the same are less likely to be effective. Are U.S. policymakers concerned about the possibility of more and more Yemenis fighting in the ongoing civil war? If so, then policymakers should focus on the factors that motivate individuals not to engage in violence. Fear of repression, for example, appears to encourage revenge attacks, especially if friends have been

Strengthening opposition to violence in theory is different from strengthening opposition to violence in practice.

assaulted by security forces in the past. These results suggest that U.S. diplomats and military officials should work closely with the Arab coalition to ensure that civilians are protected from security forces, in particular, as well as rival groups in areas under their control. This policy implication is unsurprising. It reinforces what the U.S. government has learned fighting counterinsurgencies over the past decade. The policy challenge is ensuring that partner nations apply these lessons, because the counterinsurgency battle in Yemen has fallen primarily on the Arab coalition.

Along similar lines, the findings also underscore the importance of urban centers for countering violent extremism in Yemen. Survey results suggest that urban centers represent key populations for both forms of nonradicalization, albeit in different ways. Respondents in urban centers were *less likely* to support travel overseas to fight against occupying forces and yet *more likely* to express a willingness to engage in political violence in Yemen. In many ways, these findings also make sense. Urban centers have experienced much, albeit not all, of the fighting in the current conflict. These responses therefore reflect the basic realities of urban violence in Yemen's civil war. The implications for U.S. policymakers are twofold: First, CVE programs aimed at minimizing support for foreign fighter travel overseas should focus on urban centers. The intent should be to build on existing opposition in urban areas for traveling abroad to fight and help this opposition to spread outward into more rural areas of Yemen. Second, progress made in the cessation of hostilities in urban centers should be reinforced through diplomatic means to try to encourage actors on the ground to avoid repressive security measures. This could also help to overcome the propensity for urban inhabitants to engage in political violence at higher rates than rural inhabitants, as seen in our survey results. The most obvious foci are Aden, Mukalla city, and Sana'a.

In terms of individual opposition to political violence in theory, survey participants viewed local attacks against Yemeni civilians as distinct from local attacks against foreigners. In fact, respondents articulated *greater support* for attacks against Yemenis than against foreigners. This appears to be a direct result of the civil war in Yemen. But as with the other key findings, it has important implications for U.S. policy. The finding suggests that Yemenis understand the civil war as a local conflict and, thus, have been less affected by the global rhetoric of al Qaeda or the Islamic State calling for attacks against foreign interests. We suggest that these results be verified with further research in Yemen. Specifically, policymakers should try to discern how much al Qaeda and the Islamic State have made ideological inroads into new territories under their control. That said, if the findings from this survey hold true, the policy implication is that Yemen represents less of a priority for the fight against such transregional networks as the Islamic State, at least in the near term.

Our findings also suggest that social ties—as measured by the degree of influence exerted by family, friends, religious leaders, and the like—were a significant factor driving underlying attitudes toward violence in theory. However, social ties had no clear direction of effect in explaining why some Yemenis were unlikely to actually engage in political violence. Why is that? As mentioned previously, our focus group discussants indicated that the ongoing conflict in Yemen has wrought a general distrust of social authority figures in that country. This general distrust, in turn, may have diminished the significance of social ties in Yemen when it comes to individual motivations and behavior as it relates to political violence. It represents a significant policy challenge: The U.S. government and the Arab coalition may struggle to find an abundance of "credible voices" within Yemeni society for CVE programs or even perhaps diplomatic efforts to reinforce the central government. This may limit the possibilities of what can be accomplished in the near term.

Similarly, it is not uncommon for commentators to posit that one way to deal with the problem of individual radicalization is to provide an alternative outlet for grievances.[2] Democratic reforms, in this sense, logically would allow individuals to change their circumstances without having to resort to violence. Our conceptual framework identifies this idea as a "redirected pathway." The survey questionnaire asked a series of questions on political and social activism to gauge the importance of potential redirected pathways toward nonviolence. The findings suggest that redirected pathways do not diminish a propensity toward violence. In fact, the findings suggest that Yemenis view political violence along a spectrum of political activism. This finding should reinforce a general skepticism among U.S. policymakers that democratic reforms will strengthen nonradicalization in a direct and meaningful way, absent long-term social changes.

Concluding Thoughts

In conclusion, this report answered a relatively discrete question on how the U.S. government and its partners should strengthen efforts to undermine violent extremism in Yemen. It argues that the best way to do so is to reinforce those factors that appear to motivate individuals to reject political violence, both in theory and in practice. The previous paragraphs provide concrete suggestions for policymakers to strengthen CVE programs in Yemen. But this report also has implications for wider U.S. counterterrorism policy. Over the past five years, the U.S. government has undertaken a different approach in its efforts to counter the threat from al Qaeda and the Islamic State. While the U.S. government has not shied away from unilaterally attacking terrorist leaders and operatives who pose a direct threat to the U.S. homeland, it has also let partner nations take on a greater role in counterinsurgency operations

> Social ties—as measured by the degree of influence exerted by family, friends, religious leaders, and the like— were a significant factor driving underlying attitudes toward violence in theory.

in recent years. In the case of Yemen, the UAE and Saudi Arabia (the primary countries involved in the Arab coalition) have helped to bolster the internationally recognized Hadi government in the face of internal resistance. The U.S. military has attempted to minimize its own footprint, in part, to reduce the possibility of a backlash against so-called Western occupying forces. This approach appears to be working to some degree, at least so far, in that our survey results suggest surprisingly little support for attacks against foreigners inside Yemen. Of course, events could change Yemeni attitudes in the future, particularly if civilian casualties from Arab coalition airstrikes were to persist.

Damage from an airstrike in Sa'ada City, Yemen, August 2015.

Survey and Sampling

The questionnaire for our current survey was developed by the RAND Corporation and draws largely on a similar survey conducted by RAND in the West Bank and published in 2015. The survey was administered by our local partners over May 20–27, 2016. The primary objective of this survey was to produce national estimates of individual attitudes toward political violence for adults in Yemen ages 18–64 using a probability proportional to size clustered sample. All methods, procedures, and instruments used in this study were approved by the RAND Human Subjects Protection Committee.

Clustered Sample Approach

We used a clustered sampling approach, whereby probability sampling occurred in six governorates and Sana'a that were accessible by our local partners for survey research, across 21 census EAs encompassing one urban and one rural district by governorate. The advantage of a clustered approach in terms of survey implementation, particularly in an active conflict zone, is that it allows survey implementers to interview multiple individuals within a confined geographic area to increase sample size. However, when determining the expected level of precision and power for our analyses, it is necessary to account for the fact that individuals within the same cluster EAs will exhibit some amount of dependence or similarity. This similarity reduces precision and power relative to a simple random sample of the same size that does not collect data in clusters. The intracluster correlation coefficient (ICC) describes the degree of similarity among individuals within the same cluster by comparing within-group variance to between-group variance. A large ICC indicates that there are substantial similarities between respondents within a cluster as distinct from other clusters. Large ICC estimates reduce the precision of survey estimates relative to a simple random sample, whereas small ICCs indicate that there are only marginal similarities between respondents within a cluster, and that a clustered sample will more closely resemble a simple random sample.

ICC and Margin of Error Calculations

Within-cluster homogeneity is highly contingent on the observed behavior or trait being assessed. Among our survey respondents, respondents in the same enumeration area exhibited relatively low rates of intracluster correlation in their attitudes toward violence against civilians ($\rho = 0.06$) and religiosity ($\rho = 0.08$) but higher levels of intracluster correlation in their current economic situation ($\rho = 0.14$) and willingness to engage in demonstrations ($\rho = 0.21$). This is consistent with the basic notion that geographically proximate individuals should hold more consistent attitudes on issues affected heavily by local economic and political conditions.

Based on this range of estimated ICCs ($\rho = 0.06$ to 0.21), we can compute MEs for our estimates. The ME is used to express the amount of variability in survey outcomes from a random sample relative to the entire population. Here, we use ME to evaluate whether our sample size of 1,200 adults clustered within 21 EAs will produce adequate precision on summary metrics from the survey. Ideally, we seek MEs that range from 3 to 5 percentage points, but MEs as large as 10 percentage points are also reasonable for survey studies such as this one. By definition,

$$ME = Z_{95} \times \text{standard error}$$

where $Z_{95} =$ the Z-statistic for the 95-percent confidence interval (here = 1.96) and

$$\text{standard error} = \frac{\sqrt{p(1-p)}}{ESS}$$

where *ESS* denotes the effective sample size defined below and *p* denotes the rate of endorsement for an item. Given that we cannot be certain about the rate at which survey items will be endorsed in the population, we examine MEs over a number of scenarios in which we assume different rates of endorsement that equal 0.05 (rare outcome), 0.25 (moderately endorsed item), and 0.50 (evenly split items). ME calculations shown for 0.05 and 0.25 also correspondingly show the MEs for items endorsed at 0.95 (a heavily endorsed item) and 0.75, respectively.

As just noted, when conducting a sampling strategy yielding a clustered sample, we must account for the ICC; that is, how much individuals within a cluster tend to be similar—or, stated formally, how much sampled units lack statistical independence. For a clustered sample, the ESS used in the ME calculations (and power calculations shown below) is smaller than the actual or nominal sample size (NSS; here 1,200). The ESS is the sample size needed by a simple random sample to achieve a given precision or power that, in the case of clustering, reduces the effectiveness of the nominal sample size because of clustering. The ESS is less than the actual number of observations, or NSS, in a clustered sample. Note that the difference between the NSS and ESS captures the loss of precision associated with the clustered design. More precisely, the difference equals what is known as the *design effect* (DEFF), which is derived from the ICC. The DEFF associated with a simple random sample is 1. In a one-level clustered sample such as our own (e.g., where individuals are clustered within EAs), the DEFF from clustering is greater than 1 and is defined as follows:

$$\text{DEFF} = 1 + (m_1 - 1) \times r_1.$$

This holds true if the sample is obtained from m_1 persons sampled per EA and r_1 denotes the ICC for EAs (here assumed to be equal to 0.06 and 0.21, respectively). The ESS equals the NSS/DEFF. That is, we need to use the estimate of ESS as our assumed sample size in our ME and power calculations to understand the power and precision we have in our clustered design. In calculations involving our entire sample, NSS = 1,200 and m_1 = 57. When we let r_1 = 0.06, we have an ESS = 274. While, when we let r_1 = 0.21, we have an ESS of 93, meaning we will have greater precision and power for items with lower ICCs where respondents within an EA are less similar to one another and less precision and power when respondents are more similar.

Table A.1 shows our estimated ME for the entire sample based on both ICC estimates, varied by the rate p at which the population endorses a certain measure within our sample. As the rate of endorsement moves away from p = 0.50, the ME decreases and we will have greater precision for rarely endorsed or frequently endorsed items.

Table A.1. ME Estimates at Different Rates of Endorsement for Entire Sample

	ICC = 0.06	ICC = 0.21
$p = 0.05$	0.02	0.03
$p = 0.25$	0.04	0.06
$p = 0.50$	0.04	0.07

NOTE: Estimates are based on a two-stage clustered sample of 1,200 individuals, with an assumed ICC of 0.05 at the first district-level stage of sampling.

Power Calculations

Power for this study can be viewed as our ability to find statistically significant associations or correlations between particular survey items. This study examines hypotheses about predictors of nonradicalization among Yemeni nationals, including family ties, demographic and economic background, and political attitudes. To test these types of hypotheses, we use logistic regression models that appropriately control for clustering of individuals within EAs. Thus, it is of interest for us to know the magnitude of the relationships we will be able to detect in our sample. To reflect this magnitude, we computed the minimum detectable OR that can be detected as statistically significant in our logistic regression models. An OR is a measure of association between an exposure (X) and an outcome (Y), which represents the odds that an outcome will occur given a particular exposure $(X = 1)$, compared with the odds of the outcome occurring in the absence of that exposure $(X = 0)$. As with our ME calculations above, the minimum detectable OR depends on several factors. First, it depends on (1) the ICC and corresponding ESS used to fit a model, (2) the assumed rate of endorsement for a given X (p as shown in the ME calculations above), and (3) the assumed rate of the outcome in the population. As for our ME calculations, we examine power as a function of p (the rate of endorsement for a given X in the sample) and assume ICCs of 0.06 and 0.21 for EAs. For the outcome Y, we assume a hypothetical point estimate of 50 percent because this value will always produce analyses with the least amount of power given that Y has the greatest amount of variance when it is endorsed 50 percent of the time.

Table A.2 shows the minimum detectable OR based on a desired 80-percent power assuming a type-I error rate of 0.05. As shown, we only have sufficient power to examine logistic regression models on survey items where there is a fair amount of disagreement. In general, these are medium-to-large values for ORs and suggest that we will only have power to detect significant associations where the magnitude of those associations is medium to large. This is not unreasonable for a study of this nature, particularly given the constraints

Table A.2. Minimum Detectable OR in Logistic Regression Models for Entire Sample

	ICC = 0.06	ICC = 0.21
$p = 0.05$	N/A	N/A
$p = 0.25$	2.30	5.59
$p = 0.50$	2.01	3.65

Note: Estimates are based on a two-stage clustered sample of 1,200 individuals, with an assumed ICC of 0.05 at the first district-level stage of sampling.

in survey collection in conflict zones, which necessitate a clustered sampling design, and the expected size of the relationship between key predictors and outcomes of interest.

Full Regression Results

Table A.3 shows the full regression results presented in Chapter Four. Key findings are robust to estimates (not reported) produced using multiple imputation by chained equations.

Table A.3. Why People Reject Violent Extremism in Yemen—Empirical Results

	(1) DOES NOT SUPPORT FOREIGN TRAVEL TO FIGHT OCCUPIER	(2) UNWILLING TO ENGAGE IN VIOLENT PROTESTS
Very or fairly politically active	−0.219***	−0.036**
	(0.063)	(0.018)
Very or fairly optimistic life will be better than parents'	0.004	0.031*
	(0.034)	(0.017)
No matter how hard we try, nothing in this country changes	−0.014	−0.002
	(0.031)	(0.020)
Very or somewhat concerned about future assault	0.036	0.009
	(0.036)	(0.021)
Self—assaulted by security forces in past	0.114	0.024
	(0.089)	(0.119)
Family—assaulted by security forces in past	−0.074	−0.038
	(0.064)	(0.042)
Friend—assaulted by security forces in past	0.080*	−0.075**
	(0.047)	(0.038)
Self—retaliated against by rival group in past	0.014	0.007
	(0.054)	(0.028)
Family—retaliated against by rival group in past	0.094*	0.027
	(0.052)	(0.038)
Friend—retaliated against by rival group in past	−0.204	−0.019
	(0.149)	(0.048)
Self—retaliated against by own group in past	−0.160*	0.000
	(0.097)	(0.058)
Family—retaliated against by own group in past	0.034	−0.054
	(0.075)	(0.073)
Friend—retaliated against by own group in past	0.023	0.060*
	(0.116)	(0.032)
Frequent or sporadic fighting in last two weeks	0.005	0.095*
	(0.102)	(0.052)

Table A.3—Continued

	(1) DOES NOT SUPPORT FOREIGN TRAVEL TO FIGHT OCCUPIER	(2) UNWILLING TO ENGAGE IN VIOLENT PROTESTS
Parents have great or fair amount of influence	−0.061**	0.010
	(0.029)	(0.028)
Friends have great or fair amount of influence	−0.102***	0.013
	(0.023)	(0.028)
Imams have great or fair amount of influence	−0.016	−0.012
	(0.041)	(0.018)
Religious or somewhat religious (versus not religious)	0.018	−0.010
	(0.078)	(0.019)
Boys and girls can be educated in same classroom	0.076**	0.017
	(0.034)	(0.014)
Male (versus female)	0.184**	0.009
	(0.073)	(0.030)
Primary to diploma (versus illiterate or read and write)	0.005	0.009
	(0.051)	(0.027)
BA or higher (versus illiterate or read and write)	0.043	0.006
	(0.054)	(0.022)
Full-time, part-time employed, or wage laborer (versus out of the labor force)	−0.084**	−0.016
	(0.042)	(0.024)
Unemployed (versus out of labor force)	−0.058*	0.012
	(0.035)	(0.024)
Age 35–64 (versus age 18–34)	0.047	0.022
	(0.032)	(0.018)
Urban district	0.117**	−0.091***
	(0.052)	(0.028)
Ibb	Reference	Reference
Sana'a	−0.301***	−0.040*
	(0.084)	(0.022)
Al Hudaydah	−0.469***	−0.100
	(0.113)	(0.075)
Hadramawt	−0.152	−0.158*
	(0.155)	(0.094)
Aden	−0.516***	0.023
	(0.091)	(0.021)
Ma'rib	−0.182	−0.079
	(0.212)	(0.149)
Amran	−0.100	0.032
	(0.113)	(0.023)
Observations	965	923

NOTE: Marginal effects are presented, with standard errors clustered by EA in parentheses. Statistical significance is denoted by *$p < 0.1$, **$p < 0.05$, ***$p < 0.01$.

Regression Variables and Survey Instrument Questions

Table A.4 provides the exact wording used in the survey instrument for each dependent variable and covariate in our regression models presented above. Dichotomized versions of scaled items are bolded and italicized for clarity.

Table A.4. Survey Instrument Questions

REGRESSION VARIABLE	QUESTION WORDING FROM SURVEY INSTRUMENT
Does not support foreign travel to fight occupier	I would support a friend's decision to travel abroad to assist Muslims fighting a foreign occupier. (1) strongly agree, (2) agree, **(3) disagree, (4) strongly disagree**.
Unwilling to engage in violent protests	There are many ways in which people can participate in politics. I am going to read some activities and strategies to you. As I read each one, please tell me if you would ever engage in the following activities or strategies: violent protests. (1) very likely, (2) somewhat likely, **(3) somewhat unlikely, (4) very unlikely**.
Very or fairly politically active	Do you describe yourself as: **(1) very politically active, (2) fairly politically active**, (3) not very politically active, (4) or not at all politically active?
Very or fairly optimistic life will be better than parents'	Thinking about life in Yemen overall, how optimistic or pessimistic are you that your life will be better compared to that of your parents? Are you: **(1) very optimistic, (2) fairly optimistic**, (3) rather pessimistic, (4) very pessimistic?
No matter how hard we try, nothing in this country changes	What extent do you agree with the following statement? No matter how hard we try, nothing in this country changes: **(1) strongly agree, (2) agree**, (3) disagree, (4) strongly disagree.
Very or somewhat concerned about future assault	How concerned are you about being assaulted in the future? Would you say: **(1) very, (2) somewhat**, (3) a little or (4) not at all.
Self—assaulted by security forces in past	I am going to read you some things that may have happened to you. As I read each please answer "Yes" if it has or "No" if it has not. Have you ever been physically assaulted by security forces? (1) yes, (2) no.
Family—assaulted by security forces in past	Have any of the following things ever happened to a family member? Been physically assaulted by security forces? **(1) yes**, (2) no.
Friend—assaulted by security forces in past	Have any of the following things ever happened to a friend? Been physically Assaulted by security forces? **(1) yes**, (2) no.
Self—retaliated against by rival group in past	I am going to read you some things that may have happened to you. As I read each please answer "Yes" if it has or "No" if it has not. Have you ever been retaliated against by a rival group? **(1) yes**, (2) no.
Family—retaliated against by rival group in past	Have any of the following things ever happened to a family member? Been retaliated against by a rival group? **(1) yes**, (2) no.

Table A.4—Continued

REGRESSION VARIABLE	QUESTION WORDING FROM SURVEY INSTRUMENT
Friend—retaliated against by rival group in past	Have any of the following things ever happened to a friend? Been retaliated against by a rival group? *(1) yes*, (2) no.
Self—retaliated against by own group in past	I am going to read you some things that may have happened to you. As I read each please answer "Yes" if it has or "No" if it has not. Have you ever been retaliated against by members of your own group? *(1) yes*, (2) no.
Family—retaliated against by own group in past	Have any of the following things ever happened to a family member? Been retaliated against by members of own group? *(1) yes*, (2) no.
Friend—retaliated against by own group in past	Have any of the following things ever happened to a friend? Been retaliated against by members of own group? *(1) yes*, (2) no.
Frequent or sporadic fighting in last two weeks	Coded by enumerator. *(1) frequent fighting and air strikes/ shelling causing damages, injuries or death*, *(2) sporadic fighting and air strikes/shelling causing damages, injuries or death*, (3) no fighting, air strikes/shelling, no damages, injuries or death.
Parents have great or fair amount of influence	Thinking of major decisions that affect your life (such as those related to education, work, and social activities and marriage), how much influence do each of the following have over those decisions? Would you say your parents have *(1) a great deal of influence*, *(2) a fair amount of influence*, (3) only a little influence, (4) or no influence at all?
Friends have great or fair amount of influence	Thinking of decisions that affect your life (such as those related to education, work, and social activities and marriage), how much influence do each of the following have over those decisions? Would you say your friends have *(1) a great deal of influence*, *(2) a fair amount of influence*, (3) only a little influence, (4) or no influence at all?
Imams have great or fair amount of influence	Thinking of decisions that affect your life (such as those related to education, work, and social activities and marriage), how much influence do each of the following have over those decisions? Would you say Imams/Religious leaders have *(1) a great deal of influence*, *(2) a fair amount of influence*, (3) only a little influence, (4) or no influence at all?
Religious or somewhat religious (versus not religious)	Generally speaking, would you describe yourself as: *(1) religious*, *(2) somewhat religious*, (3) not religious.
Boys and girls can be educated in same classroom	I am going to read you some statements. As I read each one, please tell me whether you: *(1) strongly agree, (2) somewhat agree*, (3) somewhat disagree, (4) strongly disagree with the statement. It is acceptable for girls and boys to be educated together in the same classrooms.
Male (versus female)	Coded by interviewer.

Table A.4—Continued

REGRESSION VARIABLE	QUESTION WORDING FROM SURVEY INSTRUMENT
Education status *Illiterate or read and write = 1+2* *Primary to diploma = 3+4+5* *BA or higher = 6+7+8*	What is the highest level of education you have completed? (1) None/illiterate, (2) Reads and writes (informal education), (3) Primary/Basic Education (Grade 1-9), (4) Diploma – Vocational before secondary level 5, (5) Diploma College Diploma – two years (Vocational/alternative), (6) BA, (7) MA or higher, (8) Other, secondary or other.
Employment status *Full-time, part-time employed, or wage laborer = 1+2+3* *Unemployed = 4* *Out of the labor force = 5*	What is your current job status? Are you currently: (1) Working/employed full time, (2) Working/employed part time, (3) Daily low-wage laborer (in agriculture, construction, etc.) (4) Not working/unemployed and looking for work, (5) Not working/unemployed and not looking for work, (6) Other
Age	How old were you on your last birthday? (1) 18–24, (2) 25–34, (3) 35–44, (4) 45–54, (5) 55–64
Urban district	Coded by enumerator.
Governorate	Coded by enumerator.

NOTE: Dichotomized versions of scaled items are bolded and italicized for clarity. Additionally, respondents who stated that their current job status was "other" were manually recoded based on clarifying information provided in each survey response.

Discussion of Weighted Results to Address Educational Differences in Sample

To account for differences between the education status of our sample and that found in the 2004 Yemeni census, we also ran a weighted version of these models to account for known population sizes by education status, governorate, and urban area. The combined effect of these models is to overweight illiterate respondents and underweight more highly educated respondents relative to the results presented in our sample.

Coefficients are not presented; however, the direction of effect of each coefficient was entirely unchanged. Beyond several changes in marginal significance of some variables, only a few changes in statistical significance at the 95-percent level exist between the weighted and unweighted versions of our model, none of which majorly affect our policy recommendations. In terms of support for a friend traveling abroad to fight, the influence of friends remains negative but is no longer significant, while respondents older than age 35 appear statistically significantly less likely to support violence abroad (this effect was not significant in the unweighted model). Urban areas are no longer significant, likely related in some form to using urban-area specific weights from the 2004 census. Effects for Amran governorate become significant.

In terms of the actual choice to engage in violence, political activity is no longer significant. This likely reflects the fact that more rural and undereducated Yemeni respondents have lesser engagement with national or subnational politics in Yemen than more highly educated and active respondents and does not refute our main findings related to the agency that violence may provide to politically active individuals in Yemen. In line with our finding that the fear of repression may serve an immediate dampening effect on violent behavior, past retaliation by a rival group significantly increases an individual's unwillingness to engage in violence, as well as negates the statistical significance of past assault by security forces on a friend which was correlated with more violence. Respondents with influential friends remain correlated with an unwillingness to engage in violence but now in a statistically significant way. Lastly, Amran becomes statistically significant in the weighted models.

Overall, none of these differences reflects adversely upon our primary findings, and in some cases even affirm key findings from unweighted models. Given the very real likelihood that the 2004 census is no longer an adequate representation of the true demographic breakdown of Yemen's population after years of population shifts and migration, further research is needed to more accurately diagnose proper weighting schemes.

Notes

Chapter One

[1] Adam Liptak, "Detainee Said to Confess Role in Cole Bombing," *New York Times*, March 19, 2007.

[2] Office of the Spokesperson, U.S. Department of State, "Terrorist Designation of Shawki Ali Ahmed al-Badani," Washington, D.C., June 17, 2014.

[3] James R. Clapper, "Statement for the Record on the Worldwide Threat Assessment, Presented to the Senate Select Committee on Intelligence," Washington, D.C., January 31, 2012.

[4] For more information, see Kim Cragin, Melissa A. Bradley, Eric Robinson, and Paul S. Steinberg, *What Factors Cause Youth to Reject Violent Extremism?* Santa Monica, Calif.: RAND Corporation, RR-1118-CMEPP, 2015; Kim Cragin, "Resisting Violent Extremism: A Conceptual Model for Non-Radicalization," *Terrorism and Political Violence*, Vol. 26, No. 2, December 2013, pp. 337–353; and Paul K. Davis and Kim Cragin, *Social Science for Counterterrorism: Putting the Pieces Together*, Santa Monica, Calif.: RAND Corporation, MG-846-OSD, 2009.

[5] For more information, see Christopher Boucek, *Yemen: Avoiding a Downward Spiral*, Carnegie Endowment for International Peace, No. 102, September 2009; Paul Dresch, *A History of Modern Yemen*, Cambridge, UK: Cambridge University Press, 2000; Gregory D. Johnsen, *The Last Refuge: Yemen, Al-Qaeda, and the Battle for Arabia*, London: Oneworld Publications, 2013.

[6] Cragin, 2013, p. 338.

[7] Cragin et al., 2015.

[8] In December 2009, Umar Farouk Abdulmutallab boarded Northwest Airlines flight 253 from Amsterdam to Detroit, intending to detonate a suicide bomb and kill his fellow passengers. While the attack was unsuccessful, authorities discovered that the relatively sophisticated bomb had been developed by al Qaeda's branch in Yemen. One year later, in October 2010, AQAP tried again; it placed bombs disguised as printer cartridges on cargo planes traveling to the United States.

[9] Cragin, 2013; Cragin et al., 2015.

Chapter Two

[1] Human Rights Watch, "Yemen: Events of 2016," undated, estimates that 4,125 civilians had been killed as of October 10, 2016. The larger estimate—of 10,000 civilians in the conflict—is attributed to the UN Office for the Coordination of Humanitarian Affairs by Ahmed al-Haj, "Yemen Civil War: 10,000 Civilians Killed and 40,000 Injured in Conflict, UN Reveals," *Independent*, January 17, 2017; one report from August 2016 estimated that upward of 6,000 fighters had been killed by that time. Mohammed Ghobari, "U.N. Says 10,000 Killed in Yemen War, Far More Than Other Estimates," Reuters World News, August 30, 2016.

[2] International Organization for Migration, "Displacement Tracking Matrix Yemen: Round 12," January 2017; Central Intelligence Agency, "Middle East: Yemen," *World Factbook*, January 12, 2017. Note that other estimates of Yemen's GDP per capita in real terms may fall well below these estimates if not expressed in terms of purchasing power parity, which accounts for the real value of a common basket of consumer goods inside Yemen.

[3] Battle deaths are estimated to be 1,200–11,000 (see "Battle Deaths Dataset Version 3.0," PRIO website, October 2009). Population estimates, inclusive of women and children, indicate that the total population of what was then the Yemen Arab Republic was approximately 3.8 million (see U.S. Department of Commerce, Bureau of the Census, *International Population Dynamics 1950–1979: Demographic Estimates for Countries with a Population of Five Million or More*, Washington, D.C., 1980).

[4] Battle deaths for the 11-day civil war are estimated to be 10,000–13,000 (see "Battle Deaths Dataset Version 3.0," 2009). Population estimates, inclusive of women and children, indicate that the total population of what was then the People's Democratic Republic of Yemen was approximately 2.3 million (see Arthur S. Banks, Alan J. Day, and Thomas C. Muller, *Political Handbook of the World 1998*, Basingstoke, UK: Palgrave MacMillan, 1998).

[5] "Battle Deaths Dataset Version 3.0," 2009; Banks, Day, and Muller, 1998.

[6] See Sarah Phillips, *Yemen's Democracy Experiment in Regional Perspective: Patronage and Pluralized Authoritarianism*, New York: Palgrave MacMillan USA, 2008, p. 9, for an example. Tribal clashes with national security forces were frequent as early as 1998 (see "Security Incidents in Yemen, 1998," al-Bab website, August 6, 2015).

[7] For additional discussion of the Houthi movement, see Barak Salmoni, Bryce Loidolt, and Madeleine Wells, *Regime and Periphery in Northern Yemen: The Huthi Phenomenon*, Santa Monica, Calif.: RAND Corporation, MG-962-DIA, 2010; and Christopher Boucek, *Yemen: Avoiding a Downward Spiral*, Carnegie Endowment for International Peace, No. 102, September 2009.

[8] The first major protest was in January 2011 in the capital city of Sana'a, with more than 16,000 protestors. See "Arab Spring: A Research Study Guide, Yemen," Cornell University Library, October 12, 2016.

[9] For a synopsis, see "Arab Uprising Country by Country: Yemen," BBC News online, December 16, 2013.

[10] The agreement for this political transition, which was backed by the GCC, was signed in November 2011 in Riyadh. This agreement granted immunity to Saleh and outlined an ambitious set of milestones, negotiations, and, ultimately, reforms to create stable political institutions in the country. For an English translation of the Gulf initiative, see "Yemen Transition Agreement, 2011," al-Bab, undated text.

[11] The National Dialogue Conference was formed by United Nations Security Council Resolution 2051 in 2012; it set out the structure of working groups and leadership tasked with planning and structuring a transitional government for Yemen. See Charles Schmitz, "Yemen's National Dialogue," Middle East Institute website, March 10, 2014.

[12] Schmitz, 2014.

[13] "Yemen Swears in New Government Amid Boycott," Al Jazeera, November 9, 2014.

[14] "Trouble Again in the North," *Economist*, November 24, 2012.

[15] Mohammed Ghobari, "Tens of Thousands of Yemeni Houthis Protest Against Government in Capital," Reuters World News, August 22, 2014; "Yemen's Capital Sanaa was Seized by Rebels," BBC News online, September 14, 2014; International Crisis Group, "Yemen: Is Peace Possible?" *Brussels, Middle East Report 167*, February 9, 2016.

[16] Mareike Transfeld, "The Failure of the Transitional Process in Yemen, the Houthi's Violent Rise to Power and the Fragmentation of the State," *SWP Comments (German Institute for International and Security Affairs)*, Vol. 6, February 2015; "Instability in Yemen: Held Hostage," *Economist*, January 24, 2015.

[17] Hakim Almasmari and Jason Hanna, "Yemen's Deposed President Flees House Arrest, Plans to Withdraw Resignation," CNN, February 22, 2015; "Beleaguered Hadi Says Aden Yemen 'Capital,'" *Business Insider*, March 7, 2015.

[18] Alexis Knutsen, "2015 Yemen Crisis Situation Report: March 22," AEI Critical Threats website, March 22, 2015.

[19] "Yemen's President Hadi Asks UN to Back Interventions," BBC News online, March 25, 2015; Ali Ibrahim al-Moshki, "Dozens Killed by Raids Under Operation Decisive Storm," *Yemen Times News*, March 30, 2015.

[20] Katherine Zimmerman, "al Houthi Areas of Influence," AEI Critical Threats website, July 16, 2015.

[21] "Houthis Seize Strategic City in Yemen, Escalating Power Struggle," *Huffington Post*, May 22, 2015.

[22] Zimmerman, 2015; Yara Bayoumy and Mohammed Ghobari, "Iranian Support Seen Crucial for Yemen's Houthis," Reuters, December 15, 2014.

[23] Michael Knights and Alexandre Mello, "The Saudi-UAE War Effort in Yemen (Part 1): Operation Golden Arrow in Aden," Washington Institute website, policy watch 2464, August 10, 2015; Ishaan Tharoor, "What Saudi Arabia Has Achieved After Bombing Yemen for a Month," *Washington Post*, April 23, 2015.

[24] "Yemen Conflict: Saudi Arabia Ends Air Campaign," BBC News online, April 21, 2015.

[25] Knights and Mello, 2015.

[26] Knights and Mello, 2015.

[27] Ahmed al-Haj, "Airstrikes Pierce New Yemen Truce Following Ground Fighting," Associated Press published on the Military Times website, July 11, 2015.

[28] Mohammed Ghobari and Noah Browning, "Yemen Peace Talks Struggle as Air Strikes Shake Truce," Reuters World News, May 8, 2016.

[29] National Counterterrorism Center, "Al-Qa'ida in the Arabian Peninsula (AQAP)," undated.

[30] National Counterterrorism Center, undated.

[31] Shuaib Almosawa, Kareem Fahim, and Eric Schmitt, "Islamic State Gains Strength in Yemen, Challenging Al Qaeda," *New York Times*, December 14, 2015.

[32] "Qaeda Kills Three in Sweep of Yemen's South," *Business Standard* online, February 20, 2016.

[33] Michael Knights, "The U.A.E. Approach to Counterinsurgency," *War on the Rocks*, May 23, 2016.

[34] Abu Bakr al-Baghdadi, "Even If the Apostates Despise Such," audio produced by the Islamic State's al-Furqan Media Foundation, November 13, 2014.

[35] H. Gambhir, *ISIS Global Intsum*, Institute for the Study of War, March 1–May 7, 2015.

[36] Gambhir, 2015; Almosawa, Fahim, and Schmitt, 2015; Ashraf al-Falahi, "Islamic State Extends Its Tentacles into Yemen," Kamal Fayad, trans., *Al Monitor Gulf Pulse*, November 30, 2015.

[37] Asa Fitch and Saleh al-Batati, "ISIS Fails to Gain Much Traction in Yemen," *Wall Street Journal*, March 28, 2016.

[38] Almosawa, Fahim, and Schmitt, 2015.

[39] "ISIL Blamed for Deadly Blasts in Yemen's Aden," Al Jazeera, May 24, 2016.

[40] Stephen Day, "The Political Challenge of Yemen's Southern Movement," Carnegie Endowment for International Peace, March 2010.

[41] For an excellent collection of key events in southern Yemen from 2010 to 2011, see Cody Curran, Nathaniel Horadam, Paul Jarvis, Matthew Lu, David Schapiro, and Miles Taylor, "Unrest in Southern Yemen," AEI Critical Threats website, August 16, 2011.

[42] Sasha Gordon, "Desknote: The Southern Movement Uprising," AEI Critical Threats, February 28, 2013.

[43] "Fatal Clashes as Yemen Protests Spread," Al Jazeera, January 24, 2015.

[44] Ali al-Mujahed and Hugh Naylor, "Yemeni Militiamen Appear to Be Driving Houthi Rebels Out of Aden," *Washington Post*, July 16, 2016.

[45] "The Latest on the Clashes in the Area of the Presidential Palace in Aden: Pictures from the Field [آخر ما وصلنا بشأن الاشتباكات الدائرة في محيط القصر الرئاسي بعدن .. شاهد "صور من الميدان"]," Mareb Press website, February 28, 2016.

[46] International Organization for Migration, 2017.

[47] "Crisis Overview: Yemen," United Nations Office for the Coordination of Humanitarian Affairs website, undated.

[48] Jason M. Breslow, "The Human Costs of the War in Yemen," Frontline, May 3, 2016; Adam Baron, "Everyone Is Losing Yemen's War," *Foreign Policy*, April 28, 2015.

Chapter Three

[1] For more information on the conceptual model and the literature review used to derive it, see Cragin, 2013.

[2] Cragin, 2013.

[3] Marc Sageman, "The Normality of Global Jihadi Terrorism," *Journal of International Security Affairs*, No. 8, Spring 2005, pp. 79–89.

[4] For more information on this difference, see Cragin et al., 2015; the discussion of the model is drawn from this report.

[5] Moderators did not report any difficulty with the focus group recruitment or sessions, despite the unrest, but the women participants did not want a voice recording of the discussions.

[6] Topic: maternal health, subnational, ten rural governorates, and more than 7,000 respondents (Abdullah N. Alosaimi, Riitta Luoto, Abdul Wahed al Serouri, Bright I. Nwaru, and Halima Mouniri, "Measures of Maternal Socio-economic Status in Yemen and Association with Maternal and Child Health Outcomes," *Maternal Child Health Journal*, Vol. 20, No. 2, February 2016, pp. 386–397); topic: judicial systems, subnational, ten governorates, and Sana'a (Erica Gaston and Nadwa al-Dawsari, *Justice in Transition in Yemen: Mapping of Local Justice Functioning in Ten Governorates*, Washington, D.C.: United States Institute of Peace, Peaceworks No. 99, 2014); topic: youth labor, internships, subnational, Sana'a, and 500 respondents (David McKenzie, Nabila Assaf, and Ana Paula Cusolito, "The Demand For, and Impact of, Youth Internships: Evidence from a Randomized Experiment in Yemen," *IZA Journal of Labor and Development*, Vol. 5, No. 1, December 2016); Glevum Associates for Foreign Policy Research Institute, 2011 Yemeni Stability Survey, March 2011; Chris Miller, Hafez al-Bukari, and Olga Aymerich, *Democracy, Political Parties, and Reform: A Review of Public Opinion in Yemen*, Stanford, Calif.: Center on Democracy, Development, and the Rule of Law, Stanford University, October 2012; Arab Barometer, "Yemen," arabbarometer.org, undated.

[7] Typically, margins of error within 3 to 5 percent are acceptable for polling in nonconflict zones. If, for instance, 50 percent of the population in our survey indicates that they are willing to engage in political violence with a 5-percent ME, we are reasonably confident that the true proportion willing to engage in political violence is between 45 percent and 55 percent.

[8] Central Statistical Organization—Ministry of Planning and International Cooperation, "Yemen General Population, Housing, and Establishment Census, 2004," International Household Survey Network website, 2004.

[9] Using similar data from the 2004 census reported in the appendix of this report, we also find that districts included in our sample are roughly comparable with those excluded from our sample in terms of population size, as well as overall levels of electrification, agricultural activity, and development. Adult male illiteracy is largely below the national average in our sample, with the exception of Al Hudaydah governorate. Estimates are not reported. To account for potential differences in education status of our population, we incorporate controls for education status in our empirical models presented in Chapter Four. We also test the robustness of our results to reweighting our sample to match national averages by education status and find few substantive differences affecting our results. See the appendix for further discussion.

[10] Doyle McManus, "Why the US Is Courting the Houthis Taking Control in Yemen," *Los Angeles Times*, February 7, 2015.

[11] Current violence levels and governorate fixed effects are the predominant statistically significant explanatory variables in a preliminary analysis of attitudes toward attacks against civilians. Regressions are not reported.

[12] This included questions asking respondents to agree or disagree with the following statements, "Our political leaders care about and listen to ordinary citizens like me"; "No matter how hard we try, nothing in this country changes"; "In this country, people are able to achieve change through their own efforts"; and "Thinking about life in Yemen overall, how optimistic or pessimistic are you that your life will be better compared to that of your parents."

Chapter Four

[1] These covariates include the variables presented throughout Chapter Three, which include binary indicators of political activism, optimism, apathy, concern over future assault; whether the respondent or respondent's family or friends have been assaulted by security forces, retaliated against by a rival group, or retaliated against by their own group in the past; whether frequent or sporadic fighting has occurred in the respondent's area in the last two weeks before survey collection; whether parents, friends, or imams have a great or fair amount of influence over major life decisions; whether the respondent is religious or somewhat religious, and whether the respondent believes boys and girls can be educated in the same classroom; as well as demographic variables including sex, education, employment status, and age of the respondent; plus geographic variables including whether the respon-

dent lives in an urban or rural district, as well as governorate fixed effects. Full survey instrument text for each question is included in the appendix.

Chapter Five

[1] Other papers in the series include the following: Cragin, 2013; and Cragin et al., 2015.

[2] See, for example, Matt Qvortrup, "Electoral Reform and Counter Terrorism," Extremis Project, October 23, 2012. That said, this idea has been refuted as far back as the mid-1970s; see Walter Laqueur, *The Age of Terrorism: A Completely Revised and Expanded Study of National and International Political Violence, Based on the Author's Classic, TERRORISM*, Boston: Little, Brown & Company, 1987, pp. 5–10.

Appendix

[1] Cragin et al., 2015.

About This Report

Why do some individuals engage in political violence in Yemen, while others do not? In this report, the third in a series on this topic, the authors examine the role that social, political, and economic factors play on individual behavior toward violence in the midst of Yemen's bloody and multiyear civil war. This report uses a unique national survey conducted in Yemen in 2016, amid active fighting, to better understand why Yemenis may reject political violence despite persistent conflict and civil unrest across the country. The report addresses how the U.S. government and its partners can strengthen efforts to undermine violent extremism in Yemen, with implications for future programs on countering violent extremism worldwide.

The authors would foremost like to thank our local Yemeni partners, who worked diligently and bravely to field this survey amid protracted fighting in many parts of the country. Their insights into conditions on the ground and expert technical advice vastly improved the quality of this report and provided much-needed nuance to our empirical findings. Additionally, the authors thank Beth Ann Griffin at the RAND Corporation for her expert guidance regarding statistical power and sampling methodology. The authors would finally like to thank Howard Shatz and Miriam Matthews at the RAND Corporation for their thoughtful reviews and guidance, which greatly benefited both the empirical and theoretical portions of this report. Any errors or omissions remain the sole responsibility of the authors.

This research was sponsored by the Office of the Secretary of Defense for Cost Assessment and Program Evaluation and conducted within the International Security and Defense Policy Center of the RAND National Defense Research Institute, a federally funded research and development center sponsored by the Office of the Secretary of Defense, the Joint Staff, the Unified Combatant Commands, the Navy, the Marine Corps, the defense agencies, and the defense Intelligence Community.

For more information on the RAND International Security and Defense Policy Center, see www.rand.org/nsrd/ndri/centers/isdp or contact the director (contact information is provided on the web page).

United Nations mobile health clinic in Follah, Sa'ada governorate, Yemen, March 2016.